SUMMER READING: CHRISTIAN CLASSICS

BY DAVID W. HALL

© The Covenant Foundation
2011

TABLE OF CONTENTS

Introduction	Remembering	3
Chapter 1	Richard Baxter's *The Godly Home*	17
Chapter 2	Thomas Watson's *All Things for Good*	29
Chapter 3	*Confessions:* Augustine's and Ours	39
Chapter 4	Luther's *The Bondage of the Will*	51
Chapter 5	Calvin and *Institutional Christianity*	64
Chapter 6	John Bunyan's *Pilgrim's Progress*	83
Chapter 7	*Contentment* (Burroughs): *A Rare Jewel*	96
Chapter 8	*Orthodoxy* (Chesterton)	109
Chapter 9	*Mere Christianity* (C. S. Lewis)	124
Chapter 10	Charles Spurgeon: *All of Grace*	138
Chapter 11	*The Sovereignty of God* (A. W. Pink)	152
Chapter 12	*The Cost of Discipleship* (Bonhoeffer)	164
Chapter 13	*The Mystery of the Lord's Supper* (Watson)	177

Introduction

Remembering

Psalm 78

Below is a brief exploration of the past and great literature and thought from the Christian tradition. From the outset, most of us would do well to agree with Lord Acton who said: "Just as loss of memory in an individual is a psychiatric defect calling for a medical treatment, so too any community which has no social memory is suffering from an illness."[1]

Many modern Christians treat the past like a dead, and therefore irrelevant, ancestor. As a result, memory has little or no place in an age that has little vision. Remembering, rather than repressing, memories about our predecessors and their virtue may be an undetected aid "for the living of these days," unless, of course, we have definitively judged that our spiritual parents were so feeble, inferior, cowardly, or unenlightened as to be prevented from communing at the same table as we. That is the arrogance of the modern.

Agreeing with Solomon that "there is nothing new under the sun" (Eccl. 1:9), Christians in all ages can instruct those who live later. We, in turn, can learn much by standing on the shoulders of those who have preceded us. After all, if the "faith was handed

---

[1] Lord Acton, cited in John Briggs, "God, Time and History," *Eerdmans Handbook to the History of Christianity*, Tim Dowley, ed. (Grand Rapids: Eerdmans, 1977), p. 2.

down once and for all" (Jude 3), one may expect little change in core biblical truths over the centuries. Since the faith is essentially the same in all centuries, surely we can learn from other brothers and sisters in Christ. We will find some agreement with Chesterton who called the church a "democracy of the dead," meaning that (for those who love popular referenda) if we truly understand the unity of the church, both militant and triumphant, we will not deliberately disenfranchise those who have gone home to be with the Lord. They, too, have much to say in the referenda of today; though they are dead, they still speak (Heb. 11:4), and we need to learn to listen. Perhaps fewer mistakes would be made if we returned free expression to those spiritual pioneers who have preceded us. The 12 [13 if optional?] titles below are primers for those of us who've come late to the party. Thankfully, we have advice to follow.

Most young adults only develop a deep appreciation for their parents when they are tested. That may be true in spiritual things as well. As one is tested by a very modern and often perplexing world, the Christian not only wants to know God's Word and will, but also on many occasions would like to ask his parents a few questions like: "What did you do when such and such happened? How did you handle a particular situation? What resources or avoidable pitfalls are available in regard to the following issues?"

The good news is that God has not left us totally without helpful advisors. Yet, frequently we do not even know they exist or where to turn for help. Much of that is our own fault or due to our over-confident unwillingness to receive advice. Often modern Christians shut themselves off from helpful sources of direction by deciding from the outset that the knowledge of previous generations is of little or no value. Although the similarity is unintended, that is not altogether different from the 1960s slogan: "Don't trust anyone over thirty."

Funny that when most of us passed that 30-year mark and started our own families, things began to change. Similarly, it may be time to admit that we can trust some earlier Christians and beliefs, those that were well thought-out and scriptural, that are centuries old. Many earlier episodes of spiritual history may benefit evangelicals, if we can merely be healed of our phobia of anything older than thirty years old. The classics re-introduced in this volume form a short course in accrued wisdom from previous giants.

The Value of Testimonies from History

One contemporary thinker recently questioned whether there was value in knowing a medieval Christian thinker. Phrasing the important question this way, he queried: "But can a seven-hundred-year-old thinker still be relevant today? Students of logic will recognize the implication of the question as the fallacy of 'chronological snobbery.' 'New is true' and 'old is mold,' we are told. Logic informs us, how-ever, that time has no necessary connection with truth. Or at least, if there were any kind of connection, then the time-honored thought ought to have the edge."[2]

An appropriate assessment of the motive and utility of remembering was summarized well by Scotsman William Symington a century and a half ago:

> The disposition to commemorate events, whether of public or private interest, springs from a law of our nature. It is true, the law has been abused,—grossly abused, for purposes of a superstitious character, . . . Nevertheless, the law is good, if men use it lawfully. . . . Matters of great and permanent utility, the due consideration of which is fitted to exert a continued beneficial influence on society, are thus held forth to the view of the community, and prevented from passing into oblivion. The very act of reminiscence itself is calculated to call into operation, and consequently to improve by exercising, some of the higher moral principles of the heart, such as gratitude for benefits received, veneration for departed worth, and imitation of praiseworthy excellence.[3]

---

[2] Norman Geisler, *Thomas Aquinas: An Evangelical Appraisal* (Grand Rapids: Baker, 1991), p. 11.

[3] William Symington, "Historical Sketch of the Westminster Assembly of Divines," *Commemoration of the Bicentenary of the Westminster Assembly of Divines* (Glasgow, 1843), pp. 31-32.

Lord Acton spoke of the past as capable of teaching by illuminating "the instructions derived from the errors of great men."[4] He also noted: "The value of history is its certainty, against which opinion is broken." If we find that our parents were on to some things that we have not realized, or if perhaps their insights were deeper than the average paperback Christian book, then we should not be so arrogant as to cling to an uncritical bias for the modern. Jeremiah spoke of the "ancient paths" (Jer. 6:16), those tried and trusted ruts of life that rebels sought to re-fill because they were routine. We may even find, as C. S. Lewis did, that some of the ancient Christian examples are preferable to many unproven modern ones. As Lewis advised of newer books and works, "A new book is still on its trial and the amateur is not in a position to judge it. It has to be tested against the great body of Christian thought down the ages, and all its hidden implications (often unsuspected by the author himself) have to be brought to light . . . The only safety is to have a standard of plain, central Christianity . . . which puts the controversies of the moment in their proper perspective. Such a standard can be acquired only from the old books. It is a good rule, after reading a new book, never to allow yourself another new one till you have read an old one in between."[5]

Lewis exhorts: "The only palliative is to keep the clean sea breeze of the centuries blowing through our minds, and this can be done only by reading old books. Not, of course, that there is any magic about the past. People were no cleverer then than they are now; they made as many mistakes as we. But not the same mistakes . . ."[6]

Nearly a century ago, G. K. Chesterton gave testimony about the value of rediscovering our past Christian heritage, when he found that the best truths had already been mined:

---

[4] J. Rufus Fears, ed., *Selected Writings of Lord Action: Essays in Religion, Politics, and Morality* (Indianapolis: Liberty Press, 1988), p. 623.
[5] C. S. Lewis, *God in the Dock* (Grand Rapids: Eerdmans, 1970), p. 201.
[6] Idem.

I did, like all other solemn little boys, try to be in advance of the age. Like them I tried to be some ten minutes in advance of the truth. And I found that I was eighteen hundred years behind it . . . . When I fancied that I stood alone I was really in the ridiculous position of being backed up by all Christendom. It may be, Heaven forgive me, that I did try to be original; but I only succeeded in inventing all by myself an inferior copy of the existing traditions of civilized religion . . . It might amuse a friend or an enemy to read how I gradually learnt from the truth of some stray legend or from the falsehood of some dominant philosophy, things that I might have learnt from my catechism,if I had ever learnt it . . . I found at last what I might have found in the nearest parish church.[7]

Lord Acton could have been helpful once again. He asked, "How is man superior to prejudice, passion, and interest?" His answer was: "By the study of History and the pursuit of the required character."[8] Moreover, he recommended an option that is often ignored: "Resist your time, take a foothold outside it, see other times and ask yourself whether the time of our ancestors is fit for us."[9]

A Theology of and Worth Remembering

Before proceeding, a set of preliminary questions deserve to be answered: Does God want us to remember the past and be encouraged by it? Why should we remember any event in a past age? Why remember? Is it helpful, or is it automatically idolatry that is wrongly focused?

A biblical study of the role of remembering in the Christian life might be helpful for many of us because at present most people are so routinely negative about the value of history. Memory and its

---

[7] G. K. Chesterton, *Orthodoxy: The Romance of Faith* (New York: Doubleday, 1990), 12.
[8] J. Rufus Fears, op. cit., 620.
[9] Idem.

beneficial effect is often taken for granted; yet nearly 300 variations of the word "remember" appear in the Bible. Notwithstanding the present arrogance toward the past, we find that remembering is not only commanded, but furthermore is a distinctively helpful tool for Christian living. Many times the great saints in the Scripture were told to remember how God had worked faithfully in their lives in an earlier day. The purpose of this memory was to remind them that God "in whom there is no shadow of turning" (Jas. 1:17) will remain faithful in the present and the future just as he was in the past. The biblical logic is that *if* God was so faithful in the past (and does not change; he is "immutable."), *then* remembering his unchanging faithfulness will spur us on to trust him in our own lives and in any struggles.

One indication of the special importance of spiritual remembering is the regularity with which this activity is ascribed to God. In the earliest books of the Bible, God selects this word to emphasize his whole-hearted care and providence for his people. God "remembered" Noah (Gen. 8:1; 9:15), Abraham (Gen. 19:29), Rachel (Gen. 30:22); to Moses, God specifically "remembers" his covenant with Abraham (Ex. 2:24 and 6:5) as a means of covenant renewal and inspiring Moses to be obedient.

God also remembers Hannah's yearning for maternity (1 Sam. 1:19); when he remembers, he does something about it, indicating that spiritual remembering is not merely a cognitive activity devoid of application. God and his people act differently if they remember. God remembers his covenant with Abraham, Isaac, and Jacob (Ex. 32:13); he also remembers the land, covenant, and ancestors who covenanted with him on earlier occasions (Lev. 26:42, 45). In David's time, God remembered his covenant (Ps. 105:8) as he did with Ezekiel (Ez. 16:60). Even at the birth of Jesus, Zechariah praises God who shows "mercy to our fathers and remembers his holy covenant" (Lk. 1:72). God himself models a lofty role for remembrance.

The Psalter has the greatest concentration of verses calling for remembrance. Several titles of Psalms are even classified as "remembering" Psalms (Ps. 38, 70). Imagine, a genre of inspired poetry whose focus was to bring to remembrance! In several instances the phrase "Praise his holy name" can be translated "Give thanks at the remembrance of his holiness" (Ps. 30:4; 97:12). God's righteousness is an enduring remembrance throughout all generations (Ps. 102:12).

Psalm 78

Nearly all of Psalm 78 is a retrospective of what God has already done in history. Either this is a pedantic history lesson, of little comfort or applicability to the struggling believer, or else it is a pattern of sanctified response. It is clearly the latter. One means of sanctification or personal encouragement is to recollect or to remember. Harking back to the Exodus wandering, Psalm 78 states that Israel "remembered that God was their Rock" (Ps. 78:35) following God's chastisement and renewed their trust in him. God also "remembered that they were but flesh, a passing breeze that does not return" (Ps. 78:39) and he extended mercy to them. Nevertheless, in their lapses, "They did not remember his power, the day he redeemed them from the oppressor" (Ps. 78:42).

God remembers his love and faithfulness (Ps. 98:3), his holy promise (Ps. 105:42), his covenant (Ps. 106:45), and his wonderful works (Ps. 111:4), while the people often fail to remember God's many kindnesses (Ps. 106:7). The Psalmist asked to be remembered by God when he shows mercy (Ps. 107:4), and David remembers God's ancient judgments or laws (Ps. 119:52). As a devotional staple, the Psalmist meditated: "In the night I remember your name [and all that it stands for], O Lord" (Ps. 119:55). When the people of God remembered better days, they wept (Ps. 137:1), and the forever-enduring love of God is associated with the "One who remembered us in our low estate" (Ps. 136:23). Remembering God and his dealings with people in history must be important in light of its prominence; at least it was for the saints in biblical ages who surpass many moderns in spirituality. If it was good enough for them, it surely is for us, too.

The Prophet Isaiah, in a time of national and spiritual decline, seemed to value remembering highly. It may even be that in those times of spiritual declension, mindful commemorations are most needed. In Isaiah 63:11, as a means of revival, God's "people remembered the days of old, the days of Moses and his people . . ." Could it be that revival might be hastened by the covenant people of God re-acquainting themselves with God's history? Though some may see mental recollection as merely an academic exercise, the biblical pages reveal an uncanny association between revival and remembering.

Later in biblical history, God called on Jacob and Israel to "remember these things" (Is. 44:21), and to rebels God said, "Remember this, fix it in mind . . . Remember the former things, those of long ago; I am God, and there is no other; I am God, and there is none like me. I make known the end from the beginning, from ancient times, what is still to come" (Is. 46:8-9). Isaiah is in continuity with Moses who had sung, "Remember the days of old; consider the generations long past. Ask your father and he will tell you, your elders, and they will explain to you" (Dt. 32:7).

God even provides concrete aids to help his people remember. The tassels with Scripture verses (not that different from a "Scripture Memory Packet") were "so you will remember all the commands of the Lord, that you may obey them . . . Then you will remember to obey all my commands" (Num. 15:39-40). In the belly of the fish, Jonah found remembering to be vital: "When my life was ebbing away, I remembered you, O Lord" (Jon. 2:7). Perhaps we should have more of this 'memorializing.' On the last page of the NT, as the remnant is revived, they found a written memorial to be helpful: "Then those who feared the Lord talked with each other, and the Lord listened and heard. A scroll of remembrance was written in his presence concerning those who feared the Lord and honored his name" (Mal. 3:16).

Perhaps the OT advice is not outdated: "Remember how the Lord your God led you. . . . remember the Lord your God, for it is he who gives you the ability to produce wealth, and so confirms his covenant, which he swore to your forefathers . . . Remember this and never forget how you provoked the Lord to anger. . . . do not be afraid of them; remember well what the Lord your God did . . ." (Dt. 8:2; 8:18; 9:7; and 7:18). To remember, therefore, is to benefit from the past.

In the NT, Peter remembers the words of the Lord (Mt. 26:7) and is cut to the heart. The disciples also remember the Lord's teaching (Lk. 24:8) and thereby grow in discipleship. Hebrews 10:32 shows the relationship between memory and courage when the Christians are told to "[r]emember those earlier days after you had received the light, when you stood your ground in great contest in the face of suffering." The aim of that remembering is to "not throw away your confidence; it will be richly rewarded" (Heb. 10:35). Thus memory aids in perseverance (10:36). Peter's epistles seem especially appreciative of the value of remembering how God has acted in the past. In fact the very purpose of Peter's second epistle is to use remembering "to stimulate you to wholesome thinking" (2 Pet. 3:1), a worthy virtue in any age. He reminds his readers of already established truths (2 Pet. 1:12), thinks "it is right to refresh your memory as long as I live in the tent of this body" (2 Pet. 1:13), and commits himself to "every effort to see that . . . you will always be able to remember these things" (2 Pet. 1:15). The presbyter knew the value of remembering in regard to spiritual growth.

The same can be said of the Apostle John. When he wrote to the faltering church at Ephesus, which was in danger of forsaking her first love, he did not tell her to forget about the past and set her sights only on current or futuristic perspectives. On the contrary the Apostle of Love urged the people to remember "the height from which you have fallen! Repent and do the things you did at first" (Rev. 2:5). Remembering is positive and necessary. Also, he called for the church at Sardis, the church that was in the terminal ward, to strengthen any remaining vital signs of spirituality. Specifically he said, "Remember, therefore, what you have received and heard; obey it, and repent" (Rev. 3:3).

In Scripture, memory is reserved for important things; it has a very important function for Christians. Specifically Christians are to:

- Remember their Creator in the days of their youth (Eccl. 12:1),as a means of calling covenant children to faithfulness amidst the hormonal revolution.
- Remember the Sabbath (Ex. 20:8) and keep it holy, as a means of spiritual renewal.
- Remember specific days, in Exodus 13:3, the people are instructed to "Commemorate this day" (Passover), and later in Esther 9:28 the deliverance of the Jews in Xerxes' time (The Feast of Purim) is to be "remembered and observed in every generation."
- Remember the Lord, in Nehemiah 4:14, as Nehemiah exhorted the people to faithfulness, he said to the nobles and officials: "Don't be afraid of them. Remember the Lord, who is great and awesome."
- "Remember Jesus Christ, raised from the dead, descended from David," Paul urged Timothy (2 Tim 2:8).
- "Remember those in prison" (Heb. 13:3); "remember the poor" (Gal. 2:10); and "Remember your leaders, who spoke the word of God to you. Consider the outcome of their way of life and imitate their faith. Jesus Christ is the same yesterday and today and forever" (Heb. 13:7).
- "Remember Me as often as you do this," said our Lord of the sacrament (Lk. 22:19).

Remembering is frequently advised; it is a thoughtful reflection on the things of God; it unites the historical past and the ethical present (Gal. 2:10; Heb. 13:3), and is a part of the renewing of our minds (Rom. 12:2). For our spiritual ancestors, remembering was a potent incentive to regain faithfulness to the Lord. Do not our churches, homes, and nations need this kind of revival, a faithful recollection of God's mighty deeds? Are we above this? If done properly with focus on God, memory of the past has great value.

If the scriptural principles of our predecessors were correct, then a remembering of those is indeed promising. Yet one must constantly preserve the balance between respecting the past . . . and worshipping the past. As long as ancestor-worship is avoided, remembering has great promise, for in so doing, one studies the providence of God, his handiwork in a particular epoch of history. Since all history is God's history, we have nothing to fear and much to gain from remembering the past as a guide for the present and the future. His-Story is useful to God's children in the church and in daily living.

The history of any church, spiritual moment, or person is a worthwhile guide. Church history is our friend, not an opposing fiend. Only the arrogance of self-centered modernism would induce Christians to despise the lessons of the past. In particular, the history of earlier episodes in church history can sound strikingly modern and have great value to guide Christians in the twenty-first century. One contemporary author, George Grant, summarized: "Remembrance and forgetfulness are the measuring rods of faithfulness throughout the entire canon of Scripture."

To fail to profit from our own history is also one of the surest paths to demise. Alexander Solzhenitsyn put it very well: "To destroy a people you must first sever their roots." This study is our commitment to avoid destroying ourselves and our children; instead, we seek to be renewed in our roots.

William Symington once helped capture the significance of remembering:

> We would not be chargeable with the enormous wickedness of forgetting that men are only what God makes them, and that to him all the glory . . . is to be ascribed. But we are, at the same time, unable to see wherein the bestowment of a due meed of praise on the memory of such . . . contravenes any maxim of sound morality, or any dictate of inspiration. We . . . have no hesitation in attempting to awaken, in the men of the present generation, sentiments of admiration and gratitude for the memory of worthies to whom all are so deeply indebted. . . .

While we claim and exercise the right of bringing these, like all other human productions, to the infallible touchstone of Revelation.[10]

Of the value of re-applying the past, Moses D. Hoge wrote:

Sometimes it is good to get free from the narrow environments of the immediate present and ascend some eminence which commands a view of ways long since trodden, and then, from what is taught in the review, learn to forecast the ever-widening way of the future. It is only by such studies that we catch the spirit of the great historic eras which have been potent in shaping the institutions of our own times. It is only when we can transport ourselves to the distant past and evoke from its obscurity the forms of its heroic men; it is only when we acquaint ourselves with the errors they combated, the difficulties they surmounted, the hardships they endured, that we can fully comprehend the character of the men who thus toiled and suffered, or appreciate the value.[11]

As observed a century ago, we would do well to affirm: "Ah, the past is never dead! All history is God's mighty electric battery charged to the full with slumbering forces which have subdued kingdoms, overturned thrones, and shaken the world to its center."[12]

In his *City of God*, St. Augustine defended the Christian church against allegations that it was the cause of the decay of the once-great Empire. Rather, Augustine placed the blame for societal decay in the eclipse of virtue in the Roman era. Specifically, he alleged that forgetting the past contributed to the downfall of an

---

[10] "Historical Sketch of the Westminster Assembly of Divines" by William Symington in *Commemoration of the Bicentenary of the Westminster Assembly of Divines* (Glasgow, 1843), 69, 71.

[11] Francis Beattie *et al*, *Memorial Volume of the Westminster Assembly, 1647-1897*, (Richmond: The Presbyterian Committee of Publication, 1897), 189.

[12] William Henry Roberts, ed., *Addresses at the Celebration of the Two-Hundred and Fiftieth Anniversary of the Westminster Assembly* (Philadelphia: Presbyterian Board of Publication, 1898), 273 (hereafter cited as *Anniversary Addresses*).

empire: "[T]he good old customs have been lost, and for so great an evil not only are we responsible but we should face judgment, like culprits fearing the penalty of death. By our own vices, not by chance, we have lost the republic, though we retain the name."[13] We would do well to recall his diagnosis in our own day.

Since this essay began with a quotation from Lord Acton, it might be fitting to allow him the last word as well. Opposed to a determinism by caprice, Acton advised that "knowledge of history means choice of ancestors."[14] He differentiated between being governed by the past as opposed to a liberating knowledge of the past. He recommended: "Live both in the future and the past. Who does not live in the past does not live in the future." Acton, who spoke of progress as "the religion of those who have none,"[15] also noted that history "gives us the line of progress, the condition of progress, the demonstration of error."[16] Of this historical perspective, Acton cheered: "If it enables us to govern the future, not live blind, and helpless, by disclosing the secret of progress and the course sailed, the nation that knows the course best and possesses the most perfect chart will have an advantage over others in shaping the destiny of man."[17]

This summer reading series, a handy introduction to great thinkers and topics from the past is dedicated to those ends, with the first chapter dedicated to one of my first teachers.

---

[13] Augustine, *The City of God* (New York: Doubleday, 1958), 75.
[14] J. Rufus Fears, op. cit., 620.
[15] Ibid., 636.
[16] Ibid., 634.
[17] Idem.

Chapter 1

Richard Baxter's *The Godly Home*: Honoring the Father While Not Too Late

Ephesians 6:1-4

In a book dedication a year ago, I acknowledged my recently deceased father as teaching me "to live within means, to avoid excessive debt, and to work."[18] Dad was beginning to decline seriously, and I was pleased to have the opportunity to acknowledge his impact on my life while he was still living.

I try not to say all that much about my family in sermons—although some of you think that I pick on Andrew too much but I'm working on that. It is certainly not the place of the pulpit in worship to extol the virtues of a human being in place of holding up Christ our Savior or God's work. Nor do I wish to speak of my father as a sinless, uncommonly spiritual man. Sometimes, however, God puts people in our lives to guide and illustrate his ways.

On this father's day 2011, I preached a sermon to our congregation to illustrate from several passages what I personally learned from Richard Hall, my father. I did not preach his funeral

---

[18] See *Calvin and Commerce* by Matthew Burton and myself (Phillipsburg, NJ: Presbyterian and Reformed Publishing, 2009), 6.

for a reason; yet I sought to honor my first and longest teacher in that sermon. As he lay dying, weak and wounded from the Fall, he still loved me. From my dad, I learned these biblical truisms that would help most of us on Father's Day:

1. Dads are called to work, serve, and provide; if they are not mushy or duplicated male versions of mothers, there is a reason and they should not be criticized as insensitive merely for having different callings or being men.
2. Dads can/should lead their families in worship attendance, raising them in the nurture and admonition of the Lord.
3. We should honor our fathers before they pass away; it does little good afterwards.
4. God is illustrated as a Father for many great reasons.

Also some of this may provide some clues into the back-story of what makes your pastor tick. It is, probably, hard to figure out from time to time.

So let me tell you what I learned from my Dad; and let us pray that we will learn to honor our parents and others while there is time.

Biography Shapes

My dad was born in November 1925 on a small farm in rural west Tennessee. He was the baby of four. He had an older brother who died of polio at 13, although we never heard much about that. Dad lived through the depression

And we heard many stories of 'beans and cornbread.' He was shaped by this.

However, he did not let that period of scarcity prevent him from sharing or giving. His family lost their farm during the Depression, moved to Memphis, both for jobs and for better health care for the sick brother, Billy.

He eventually attended the high school that Elvis Presley later did (Humes High School; a decade earlier) but dropped out. I think dad had education through about the 11th grade. I probably received my intellectual aptitude from him.

He joined the Navy (with his older brother) to serve his country in 1943. He trained in San Diego, but while his brother went to Okinawa, Dad was sent to guard the Panama Canal Zone and drive generals around in New Orleans. He was not a war hero, but he surely volunteered to serve and loved his country. Dad was honorably discharged in 1945.

Dad returned to Memphis and attended the University of Memphis (where Ann and I later met) on the GI bill, beginning in 1946. He first had to pass his high school equivalency (GED) and struggled as a student throughout. He was the first member of his family to graduate from college.

He wooed my mother, who had just graduated from High School. Dad was 22, and she was 18 when they married. He and mom were married in 1947 and enjoyed 64 yrs (4 days short) of marriage.

He graduated from college in 1950. Several of his classmates went on to found successful businesses.

My sister and I were raised in a family, located between *Ozzie and Harriet* and *the Wonder Years*, just before *Mad Men*. America, in the early 1950s, after the victories of War and the beginning of technological development, was a land of plenty. My dad was willing to take risks, begin a new career, and work hard.

He was a lifelong Methodist until about 1980 when he joined Independent Presbyterian Church in Memphis. Sometime in the 1950s, Dad experienced a conversion.

The pastor then was a fine Methodist evangelist, Wayne A. Lamb. I was given my middle name after this Methodist preacher. Later, Dr. Lamb almost steered me to Asbury seminary in the mid 70s, and encouraged me to be a pastor.

My dad had fairly fixed social and political ideas. He would drive academics crazy. Dads, you will pass these on, either inspiring imitation or producing revulsion among your children as Ephesians 6 teaches. He was often glued to the old black/white TV set (with 3 channels) in the 1960s, as our family watched as TV spectators: the Bay of Pigs, JFK's assassination, the Civil Rights struggles, the first man on the moon, numerous Ed Sullivan programs (Beatles), and Walter Kronkite nightly. Some of you may remember a VP in the 1990s from Tennessee by the name of Al Gore. Long before that, I became quite acquainted with his father, a Senator from Tennessee, as I often heard my dad call him by his full name: "That communist Al Gore [Sr]." I thought AlGore was his last name, communist his middle name, That his first. After WW2, Dad had already voted for Strom Thurmond as a Dixiecrat in the 1948 presidential election. I don't know where I got my conservative political leanings. But that's one of my points.

We learn tons from our fathers. It may only be much later in life that we realize such, but Dads (and moms) can have an enormous shaping influence in worldview and in spirituality. Fathers, this morning are you teaching your children a full-orbed Christian world view and the whole counsel of God? Or are you too busy with your career, self, or a hobby?

I also learned to love the St. Louis Cardinals, as we listened to radio broadcasts by the 100s. And the Memphis Tigers, who could never beat the evil University of Tennessee. Even as a young child—like many of yours—I was catechized to despise all things orange—and maybe not even for the purest of reasons. Dads, are you influencing your children for Christ and His ways as much as you are producing devotees for the dawgs, tigers, or Tide? Shouldn't you use at least as much time for something of eternal significance, say starting with being in the Lord's house every Lord's Day?

Dad taught me how to play baseball. He tried to teach me how to run—that was not too successful. He pitched to me, and to this day I love seeing dads pitching with sons. And throwing footballs. And shooting baskets—we mounted one on the back of the house. It may explain certain poor basketball techniques if every layup required one to smash into the back, brick wall of the house. We also wrestled a good bit, until a weightlifting teenager tossed dad a little hard and cracked his ribs. A generation later, 7-year old Andrew would crack granpa's ribs playing football. My son now tells me that he cannot wait until the next generation does that to me.

For over a thousand Sundays growing up in Dad's home, he never gave us the option of going to church and Sunday School. In our high school years, even if we spent the night out, we were expected to be at church next morning. Although we never theologized about it, Dad must have thought that God spoke through his Word in worship. Certainly not the biggest saint in history, still Dad never missed taking his family to the Lord's House on his day. There were plenty of other times for many other things. Isn't that part of what Ephesians 6 teaches dads?

My father even joined the choir to sing with my mom for a while. And from the choir loft, his glare could find my sister or I misbehaving in the balcony like the earliest laser beam. If that didn't work, he'd clear his throat or cough, and we knew we would be in trouble when we got home.

Speaking of which, discipline was never doubted from my dad. Dad always told us that if we got in trouble at school, no matter what was going on, there would be a spanking or consequences at home. *Teachers must have been infallible back in that day.* Or else, my dad was wise enough to know that his little "precious" was . . . not really that precious. Amazingly, my dad did not presume the sinlessness of his own children. And if we talked back or did something wrong or came in too late, there was never any doubt that something would be taken away.

Dad knew that it was part of his calling to nurture and admonish us. He warned us (and supported these) by actions:

- If you spend all your money, you'll have to stay home.
- Money doesn't grow on trees.
- Don't ever talk to your mother that way again.
- Wishing so, doesn't make it so, does it.
- If a frog had wings, he'd bump his rump when he flew.

My father's work career was all with one employer, after the Navy. He worked in the business end for the Memphis newspaper.

To stay with one employer for almost 40 years, in any decade, takes perseverance, loyalty, hard work, and other things. He received small lapel pins for 25 years, 30 years, and 35—small tokens but signs of character.

What I learned from my dad about character

* Good character will be vindicated, even if slandered. Not all people were fans of my dad. Anytime a strong male acts and takes positions, not all will like that. But I knew him to be honest, loving, loyal, and hard working. Our children each grew in their love of Granpa.

* The value of hard work and going hard after goals. He never seemed to be able to understand why an athlete, student, or worker would not use his talent to the fullest. Always go for the top prize; don't settle for second. There's really no reason to do so.

* Competitiveness is good. My dad always liked to win, even if it was playing a hand of cards or Monopoly around the family table. In fact, until his waning months he might have tried to invent a word or two at Scrabble.

Dad struggled with an ugly disease for some time. Some confused it with orneriness—and there was some of that in my dad. I probably got that gene, too.

He is now free of that. He was a regular guy. When he agreed to do something, his word was his bond. He sacrificed for his family. He did the best he could with the abilities given. He trusted his Savior.

And—shocker for some of my friends—his favorite hymn was "In the Garden," which I heard many times on Sun Am from him singing in the shower. And whether on key or not: Dad would belt it out.

When I proposed to Ann in May 1980, dad was the first person we told. He nearly teared up: "Oh, son, that's the best thing that will ever happen to you." He was correct and was my best man because he was better than all the others I knew.

He had a short temper at times; at times, he let his actions avoid the mind's filter.

For some reason he was proud that his son was a minister—likely because of his own conversion in the 50s. He was present at my ordination in 1980 and last present here last July for Andrew's wedding.

He paid for my education—$2,000 for the entire undergraduate program!

I am very grateful for the father God gave me. He cared for me, loved me, and taught me much. I believe my dad was part of the providence of God spoken of in Romans 8:28 below. Like many of us, I wish he were here so I could thank him again.

Life Lessons from another Generation

1. Don't wait until too late to speak encouragement to your dads. Most of them work hard, toil long, and give much. Sure some become slightly coarsened because they toil amidst Adam's thorns and thistles in the sweat of their brows. But they provide. Thank them for that. Don't underestimate that gift!

Also, this applies to any other relationship: don't spend all your life criticizing, blaming, and comparing your family members. Maybe thank them, honor them, and support them for what they do. What a tragedy to learn of one's admiration and love, only after this life.

2. Dads, lead your homes in worship and disciple your children. Start as young as possible. As children grow, so does their sense of independence. They won't always listen to their fathers, they won't always spend 100s of hours listening to sports events with you, they won't always take note of your political or religious views. Use those times.

Richard Baxter, in *The Godly Home*,[19] calls for fathers to guard the home and make sure that as part of overseeing discipline there is no ungodly entrance into the family, to correct, and also to cast out the ungodly (75). Fathers are also not to lose their authority by "not using it. If you suffer children to be in control [and to determine the family structure] your government will be but a name or image. A moderate course between a lordly rigor and a soft subjection or neglect of exercising your" leadership will best preserve your legacy. Also "do not lose your authority by too much familiarity. If you make your children playfellows or equals and [treat] them as your companions," they will quickly conform you to their childish customs, and "though another may govern them, they will scarce endure to be governed by you but will scorn to be subject where they once had been equal." (101)

Parents, be parents; stop trying to be buddies or to gain the favor of your children. Also, if you hope to nurture and lead your children, make sure that you are at least doing those things yourselves. "Learn first to command yourselves. Can you ever expect to have others more at your will and government than yourselves? Is he fit to rule his family in the fear of God and a holy life who is unholy and fears not God himself? Or is [a father] fit to keep them from passion, drunkenness, gluttony, or lust or any sensuality who cannot keep himself from it? Will not [children] despise such reproofs, which are contradicted in your own lives? You know this is true of wicked preachers; is it not as true [of fathers]?" (103) Fathers, do not embitter your children by hypocrisy; fatherhood is a high calling. Better to have a dad like I had who did not boast of his spirituality and showed it some than one who advertises himself as a spiritual giant while in reality is a dwarf.

Fathers, hear Richard Baxter on this: "If God does not govern your families, who shall? The devil is always the governor where God's government is refused." (105)

Let me share a few motives for dads to disciple/govern their children (from Baxter's fine work):

---

[19] Richard Baxter, *The Godly Home* (Wheaton: Crossway, 2010); quotes in parentheses taken from this edition.

1. God has ordained and uses families as a large part of his work to spread the gospel and build the church; conversely, if not believing, families may aid the Devil.
2. Families often rise and fall together, like ships; an ungodly family normally spreads that rebellion to each member.
3. A godly family tends toward security, pleasure, peace, and joy.
4. Holiness in the home tends to be passed down, not always but often.
5. "A holy, well-governed family prepares for a holy and well-governed church." (109) Dads, do you really want to help your church? Then cultivate the seeds God has given you at home.
6. Well discipled homes contribute to the state, to education, to business, and to the community. Want to fix things like the teaching of evolution, promiscuity? Don't let the church do everything—teach your own, resource yourself to lead children.
7. Homes governed well by dads are great for outreach and evangelism: show the world!
8. "Lastly, consider that holy, well-governed families are blessed with the presence and favor of God. They are his churches where he is worshipped, his houses where he dwells. He is engaged by love and promise, to bless, protect, and prosper them. It is safe to sail in the ship that is bound for heaven, for Christ is the pilot. But when you reject his government, you refuse his company, condemn his favor, and forfeit his blessing by despising his presence, interest, and commands." (112)

Train them when young! Men, God has appointed you to be the first teachers of God's Word and ways to your children. Ministers or other teachers may be strangers, but your children know you, your love, your sacrifice, your hard work. They'll listen to you. But don't wait or delegate. They won't rise up in defiance when young. They will presume you to be truthful, unless you give them reason to think otherwise. What a profound advantage! Are you using this for the kingdom? Drop everything and get this right before it is too late.

In Ephesians 6:1-4, children are commanded to honor their parents. This is not a new command but goes all the way back to Sinai, as the 5th commandment. And it is a commandment with promise.

As with most biblical commands, the duties are reciprocal. If children are to obey parents, the superiors are charged as well. In this case, fathers are given 2 clear duties: (1) a negative one, do NOT exasperate your children. That means that fathers should not set the bar so high that none can make it, or ignore age appropriateness. Nor are fathers to be the kind who will never compliment or encourage—only speaking the negative. Fathers, God commands you not to be a critic, nor to be a task-master. Do not exasperate or discourage your children. God points that out so that you'll watch that.

(2) Then the positive command is to bring them up in the training and instruction—or nurture and admonition—of the Lord. Dads are to train and disciple their children. You are their first appointed mentors. Also disciple them in the admonition—lit., to put into minds or call to their attention—the Lord's ways and words. Fathers, you are to mentor and also to speak correction to your children.

The Fatherhood of God . . . in Christ's words

Our Lord addressed God as "Father" most often in his prayers. During his times of torment and struggle, he knew his father. He portrayed God in parables as a loving Father who:

- Threw a lavish wedding banquet;
- Forgave the Prodigal son, welcoming him back in true repentance.
- And in Matthew 7 depicts a normal father as wanting to provide good things for his children, like bread and eggs, even before we ask.

God is greater than any depicted father, in Ephesians 3 and elsewhere.

Interestingly, almost everyone has a story similar to mine. Joe Fowler, a fellow elder nearby and Moderator of our presbytery recently told me that one of the hardest days of his life was laying his father to rest. Dick Dabney, a board member of Westminster Theological Seminary, told me that he still misses his father. One church member, Dr. Leon Combs, remembers his dad's death 23 years later. Many others remember.

Irfon Hughes, a retired Welsh pastor wrote recently:

> *Dear David and Ann,*
>
> *Be assured of our prayers at such a difficult time as this. Obviously we have been through all of this with both our parents and my stepmother as well.*
>
> *My father was the last parent to die, which happened just 6 years ago. I still miss my dad, mainly because we are of our father's lineage, and although emotionally we are close to our mothers we are always as men modeling our fathers. It is no accident that Father is the great revelation of God in the NT. We will pray for you . . . that you might know the great peace and grace of our heavenly Father at such a time as this."*

God is our Father for a reason!

Say what you want to your father now. Ecclesiastes 12 tells us to remember our Creator in the days of our youth. While there is time, certain things should be done. Jesus, too, advised us to do things while it is daylight.

Today, please take those opportunities to honor your dads before it is too late. And this honor extends to all in authority over you.

More importantly: say what you want to your heavenly father . . . Will you honor God today as your Father? Richard Baxter's *The Godly Home* is a help.

Chapter 2

Thomas Watson's *All Things for Good*

Romans 8:28

I was a brand new Christian the first time I heard this verse. Almost 40 years ago, I heard some mature Christians talking about this, and it revolutionized the way I saw life. Most Christians have to learn sooner or later that all will not fall out according to their plans or expectations. It is fairly easy (even though deceptive) to walk with Christ, to look to him, to trust him joyfully, when all goes well. When you win an award, get the job, get the girl, succeed in life, or triumph in a competition, all things are fine with you.

It is when we are faced with defeat, death, despair, or disappointment that this magnificent verse comes into play. And every Christian must learn to follow God in the difficult days as well as the triumphant ones. That is part of the biblical realism from the previous passage in Romans.

This remains one of my all-time favorite verses—and I know that is true for many others. And one of my favorite puritan authors wrote a book on this one verse. I'd love for each of you to read *All Things for Good* by Thomas Watson (Banner of Truth Trust [orig 1633; rpr 1986] in the Puritan paperback series for the cost of lunch). In this summer reading series, I'll take a great classic (page references in parentheses) and seek to encourage you with it.

This mammoth verse states:

1. The glorious privilege—all things work for good.

Our Lord has not given us a paltry inheritance but one that soars. It is a glorious privilege to know, prior to facing any thing, that God will work all things together for his good. The universe is not a blind God; no, our Lord is sovereign and he is so brilliant and competent as to manage the affairs of billions of people at the same time and to make all threads produce a wonderful weave.

2. The persons who receive this privilege—are doubly specified as 'lovers of God' and 'called.'

This verse may not properly be the property of all persons. Its promises belong to those who are called and who love God. First, today, make sure, you are one of those.

3. The origin and spring of this effectual calling = 'according to his purpose.'

It is the eternal counsel of God that drives and weaves this grand plan.

Before we dive into application, recall a few things about the structure of this verse.

- The subject and Actor is God. It is he, not we, who makes all things work together. This article of faith reminds us that God's work is always more important than the best of ours. God works; he's not retired.
- He works ALL things; there is no part of your life nor the universe that eludes him. And his sovereignty extends to all things—even things we were not expecting.
- God works things together for good. We ought to learn to make provisional judgments until all facts and matters are in. Sometimes things start off bad but end up good. If you are tempted to make hasty judgments, based only on partial data or initial impulse, let this

become a major part of your understanding. Learn not to be so reactionary as to be baffled by every report. Things that seem so ill at first may actually be for God's good and part of his plan. And vice versa.

- God has a special concern and love for his own children.

This single verse has great application; let's look at some with Watson as our guide.

The **certainty of this privilege** is not wavering or doubtful: we KNOW. This is not a vague guess or hypothesis: "The Spirit of God imprints heavenly truths upon the heart as with the point of a diamond. The Christian may know infallibly that there is an evil in sin, and a beauty in holiness." (10) The Lord does not sentence his people to confusing uncertainties—his promises are clear and strong. God wants you to know these truths; that's why they're set down in writing.

Next, note the **excellency of this privilege**—all works together for the good. This phrase 'work together' refers to medicine. If my daughter the pharmacist were practicing in the first century, she would use this term. "Several poisonous ingredients put together, being tempered by the skill of the apothecary, make a sovereign medicine and work together for the good of the patient. So all God's providences, being divinely tempered and sanctified, work together for the best to the saints." (11) thus we do not kill ourselves with worry but trust in God's medicine. Can you see his hand mixing the remedy in your life? Don't some of the things that taste so bitter at first end up being quite medicinal? God works all these together into a healing balm.

Note how all: THE BEST THINGS WORK FOR GOOD TO THE GODLY

1. God's attributes work for good to the Godly.
   a. God's power works for good
      i. In supporting us in trouble—"Underneath are the everlasting arms" (Dt. 33:27)

        ii. In supplying our wants. "God creates comforts when means fail." (13)

       iii. In subduing our corruptions

       iv. In conquering our enemies.

  b. God's wisdom works for good. He is not only the mighty God but also the Counselor. When we are in the dark, God brings light. "God's wisdom is the pillar of fire to go before and guide us." (14)

  c. The goodness of God works for good to the Godly. It brings common and crowning blessings.

2. The Promises of God work for good to the Godly. The "promises are notes of God's hand. He gives promises to remedy our guilt, our defilement, when we are in trouble, in want, and at all times. God's promises are "food for faith; and that which strengthens faith works for good. The promises are the milk of faith." (17)

3. The mercies of God work for good to the Godly. His mercies humble us. "The mercies of God make a sinner proud, but a saint humble. The mercies of God have a melting influence upon the soul; they dissolve it in love to God. God's judgments make us fear him, his mercies make us love him. The mercies of God make the heart fruitful and thankful. Every mercy is a balm of green grace, and this enlarges the soul in gratitude." (18) "The mercies of God quicken. God argues from the sweetness of mercy to the swiftness of duty. The mercies of God work compassion to others. Spiritual mercies work for the good—by the word preached, God's word becomes soul-transforming. Prayer becomes a 'key that unlocks the treasury of God's mercy. Prayer keeps the heart open to God, and shut to sin; it assuages the intemperate heart and the swellings of lust.' (19) Prayer sanctifies mercy, dispels sorrow, and is the Christian's weapon against the enemy. Also the Lord's Supper conveys God's mercies by quickening our affections, reviving our hope, mortifying our corruption and increasing our joy.

4. The graces of the Spirit work for good. "Grace is to the soul, as light to the eye, as health to the body. In contrast to fear, faith "keeps the heart cheerful; fear keeps the heart serious. Faith keeps the heart from sinking in despair, fear keeps it from floating in presumption." (20)

5. Angels work for the good of the saints—the "whole hierarchy of angels is employed for the good of the saints . . . they are our life-guards" (21)

6. The communion of Saints works for good. Christians are like stones in an arch to strengthen on another.

7. Christ's intercession works for good. "When a Christian is weak and can hardly pray for himself, Jesus Christ is praying for him; and he prays 3 things. First that the saints may be kept from sin (Jn. 17:15); second for his people's progress in holiness (Jn. 17:17), and third for their glorification (Jn. 17:24). "When Satan is tempting, Christ is praying! This works for good. Christ's prayer takes away the sin of our prayers. Christ . . . picks away the weeds, the sin of our prayer, and presents nothing but flowers to his father." (23)

8. The prayers of Saints work for good to the Godly. Our prayers prevail and work for others.

But this verse, as I've already indicated, does not apply only to good things.

Note also how all: THE WORST THINGS WORK FOR GOOD TO THE GODLY

Of course, bad things are the fruit of the curse. But God overrules and uses these. There are "four sad evils [which] work for good to them that love God."

1. The evil of affliction works for the good to the godly. Yes, God afflicts, and to those who are loved and called by God, these afflictions are medicinal. Afflictions are needed. No golden object is beautiful without the furnace of affliction.

Job, Joseph, Jacob, Paul—all were refined by their afflictions. Affliction works for good:

    a. Afflictions serve as our preacher and tutor. As Luther said, we never rightly understand the Psalms until we are in affliction. "A **sick-bed often teaches more than a sermon. Affliction teaches** us to know ourselves. In prosperity we are for the most part strangers to ourselves. God makes us know affliction that we may better know ourselves—and see our corruption (27)

    b. Afflictions are the means of making the heart more upright. In prosperity, we are divided—between heaven and earth. Afflictions correct us and refocus our calling.

    c. Afflictions conform us to Christ.

    d. Afflictions are destructive to sin. By degrees, Affliction works the corruption out of our hearts. It is the medicine God uses to cure us.

    e. Afflictions are the means of loosening our hearts from the world. God wants us weaned from dependence on this world.

    f. Afflictions pave the way for comfort.

    g. Afflictions yield happiness and "silence the wicked." (31) They also prepare us for glory. God uses afflictions!

Does this not change the way you view all things?

Does this not mean that we embrace even illness as from the Lord?

Shouldn't you start to view all things, even things that are not your preference or will as from the Lord?

2. The evil of temptation is overruled for good to the Godly. Satan baits us, tries to tempt us with beauty or our weakness. He presents temptations often when we are weakest. He uses the pretense of religion and any other tool. Still, God uses these temptations to reduce our pride,

to remind us of who owns us, to prove our sincerity, and to work humility often. Temptations call us to bravery, and the saints would rather die than yield to sin. When tempted, we also can comfort others, and know our limits. This leads to more prayer, too.

3. The evil of desertion works for good to the Godly. Sometimes, the Lord withholds his grace, and that is intended to draw us back to him. When a child of God wanders from God and misses that, it shows his genuine adoption. Desertions cure us of inordinate affection to the world and "makes the saints prize God's countenance more than ever." (41)

4. The evil of sin works for good to the Godly. "The sins of others . . . produce holy sorrow." (44) The sins of others lead us to feel for others and also to love grace more.

When we sin, it is as if we take a candle and begin to explore our own dark hearts. We stop flattering ourselves (49) and begin to judge ourselves more than other. "It is dangerous to judge others, but it is good to judge ourselves." (50) We will have a stricter eye on our own sin than on others.

All of these things are under the providence of God. It is our God who works these things together—"Things do not work of themselves, but God sets them working for good." (55) We should learn to see God's hand in all these things and "to adore providence." (56) "When God lays men upon their backs, then they look up to heaven." (56) God "can make the worst things imaginable turn to the good of the saints." (60) Thus, we should not be discontented with outward trials and emergencies. All things shall work for good. There are no sins that God's people are more subject to than unbelief and impatience. We faint through unbelief and fret through impatience. Discontent in an ungrateful sin, because we have more mercies than afflictions; and it is an irrational sin because afflictions work for good." (61) When we fret we may be readying ourselves to take matters into our own hands and do evil.

Instead, God wants us to be content and thankful—thankful, even in affliction. While, if even the worst things work for the good to a believer, what shall the best things—Christ and heaven—bring?

So, do we love God? Do you, this morning love God? Warm to him? Care for his wants and purposes? If not, beware. And how can we tell if we truly love God? Thomas Watson finds 14 signs or fruits of true love for God. Review these and apply:

1. The musing of the mind upon God (74)—he is our delight, our preoccupation. Do we contemplate Christ and his glory?
2. The desire of communion. "Love desires familiarity." If you can be away from God and his worship often, try the same with a human spouse.
3. Grief over sin and unkindness to God. Have I been disloyal? Disingenuous? "Does one love his friend that loves to do him an injury?" (76)
4. Magnanimity. Our hearts become valorous, courageous, when swollen with true love for God. "Love animates a Christian; it fires his heart with zeal, and steels it with courage." (77)
5. Sensitive—to his honor. We do not want to dishonor him, we 'grieve to see his glory suffer.' (77)
6. Hatred against sin
7. Crucifixion—Gal. 6;14 says it well
8. Fear—of displeasing God
9. If we are lovers of God, we love what God loves—His word, his Sabbath Day, his laws, "his image shining in the saints." (81)
10. We entertain good thoughts about God.
11. Obedience, even in difficult or dangerous things.
12. Endeavoring to make God appear glorious in the eyes of others. We will be commending and setting forth the excellencies of God.
13. Longing for Christ's appearing.

14. Stooping for the humblest areas of service—not looking for great recognition but for the humble grace to "visit the sick, relieve the poor, and wash the saints' wounds." (87)

"Happy are they who can find these fruits of love to God, so foreign to their natures but growing in our souls."

Aren't there many ways that you have seen this lately? Or will you? For example:

1. Over the next seven days, see how many times you can apply this verse. Take it with you, memorize it, apply it over and over again. It will not grow stale.
2. Talk to one another more with this. For the coming week, see if we can remind our church friends that God is working all things together. He is never off his throne. Wouldn't it help most of our friends to hear this more?
3. Use this to ward off panic!! Don't think that the world is about to end; instead, know that God uses all things.
4. Focus on affliction; learn to see that as his tool.
5. Get this little book and read it; or anything by Thomas Watson
6. This is the conclusion of Romans 8:1. There is no condemnation, but in between there is suffering. But amidst all the suffering, God orchestrates all things for good, for the good of those who love him!

The Christian may have great assurance of his salvation because of what Christ has done for us on the cross. Once the price is paid, there is no double jeopardy—since Christ bore my condemnation, there is none for me. Enjoy assurance of salvation. And the Father sends his spirit to dwell in us, to live in us, to work in us. If all that is true, then we interpret life's smaller events against this backdrop and all things work together, as a medicinal compound, for God's good.

Nothing takes God by surprise or outside of his sovereign superintendence. Nothing can happen to distort or destroy God's purposes for his people. Do you grasp that?

Whatever anyone does to you, allows you to smile. For any who attack you are also instruments of our heavenly father. Do you know that? And it is not that "things work themselves out." No, it is God himself who works these things out. God's hand intervenes in your life. If you object to that, you object to the most loving intervention possible.

God knows what you need. And he gives it. Ligon Duncan comments: "God uses every event of our lives for the express good of his people. It's not only that there's a future hope that's certain for you, it's not only that the spirit intercedes, it is that every event in your life is used by God to work for your ultimate good. Paul is saying in this grand declaration that even our messes are used by God for our ultimate good."

This is not just a mechanistic principle in the universe. This is a specific activity of the sovereign God on behalf of his children whom he has drawn into a saving relationship. It is only for believers. It's only for those who have trusted and rested in Jesus Christ. We cannot assure unbelievers with these words. For the unbeliever, for the one who has rejected God, for the one who does not trust in the Lord Jesus Christ I cannot say this suffering will result in an indescribable weight of glory. This suffering will surely be followed by the completion of God's purposes in you. I cannot give that comfort. For this promise is only made to believers.

Calvin noted that though believers and unbelievers alike are "indiscriminately exposed to similar evils, there is yet a great difference; for God trains up he faithful by afflictions, and thereby promotes their salvation."

I receive an email from two of our church members, who are dealing with a serious illness—Lou Gherig's disease. They thank God for what the Lord is doing in the wife's health. But she is struggling mightily with an illness. Here's what I share from it: "We thank you for the wonderful prayer support ____ has received. We rest on God's promises—I have been particularly encouraged by Romans 8:26-28. Though we don't see clearly now, we KNOW that this trail is ultimately for our good and his Glory." Is that not what

Paul writes here? Don't all believers need to know and benefit from this? Thomas Watson may introduce you to the classic, but the Lord calls us all to the practice in Romans.

Chapter 3

Confessions: Augustine's and Ours

James 5:16; 1 Timothy 6:12-13; Proverbs 28:13; 1 John 1:9

Mention the word "confession" in evangelical circles and someone will likely accuse you of heading Rome-ward. Confession is largely associated with Roman Catholics, but it is far too biblical to be the exclusive possession of one denomination. It is to our own loss that the activity of confession is ignored in many Protestant circles.

Confession is frequently thought of as a vestige of an earlier day, when people needed someone tangibly to confess to. However, this is hardly outdated.

Recently, I had a minister phone me. As we were talking about other things, he began blurt out his recent episode with some sin. Before I knew it, he was telling me far more than I wanted to hear, but I couldn't stop him. He was determined to confess his sin to someone, even if he had about the least likely priest possible on the phone. As I listened—helpless to halt his soul purgation—I started thinking about this. We really do need to confess our sins to others from time to time. Not that any person can remit our sins, to be sure, but sometimes we need to get it off our chest.

Don't you need that at times? When consciousness of sin is great, the need for confession is palpable.

I think the Bible expects this. Early on in NT times, James 5:16 stated, "Therefore confess your sins to each other and pray for each other so that you may be healed." This verse is in the context of calling for the Elders to pray for someone. There may even be a connection between physical healing and confession of sin in some cases. Whatever the interpretation, it is clear that in some contexts, confession of sin is legitimate and useful. And the confession in view here is more than mere confession to God; it was also confession to 'each other.' Of course, no human priest can assist or grant remission of sins. Only God can.

Maybe there is a need for a renewed appreciation of confession today. Richard Owen Roberts, a student of the history of revival, even concludes that a sure sign of true revival is when congregations freely and corporately confess their sins. That did happen in the OT at the time of Josiah, Ezra, and others. Of course, if we had that, we wouldn't have as many of those tell-all group therapy sessions, where everyone tells some ever-so-slight sin.

Let me give you 6 quick reasons why confession is shunned in Protestant churches:

1) As I've already mentions, many evangelicals avoid confession because it is associated with something that Roman Catholics do, and therefore it is assumed that everything they do is wrong. However, remember Roman Catholics affirm many of the cardinal truths of Christianity; indeed they believe more like we do than do liberal Protestants, Unitarians, and man-centered evangelicals. We should be able to appreciate a biblical practice and not dismiss it merely because it is associated with some other denomination.

2) Pride on our part is another reason we eschew confession. The essence of confession is to admit that we are wrong. It is almost a rule: the more successful a person is, the less likely it is that such person enjoys confession of sin. We hate to admit that we are wrong. That general tendency is one reason why confession is not popular.

3) Rationalization on our part is related to this. The cousin of pride is rationalization—that art which seeks to convert evil into good.

We speak of 'errors of judgment,' and mistakes. "We do admit that we make mistakes, though we [chalk them up] or put them down to weakness rather than willfulness. We apologize for our infirmities, and rather excuse than accuse our own hearts."[20] We don't mind admitting trivialities, but it is hard some-times to get Christians to admit to sin.

Rationalization is the enemy of confession. Watch this tendency in yourself.

4) Generality on our part. If we can keep things fairly generic, we don't have to focus on our own shortcomings.

"People make a general confession such as, 'I am a great sinner, 'while they would still resist any special charge brought home to their consciences, however true. Say to such a person who admits, "We're all sinners," 'you are a thief,' and he replies, 'no, I am not.' What then are you, 'a liar?' 'Oh not; Are you a sabbath breaker? "No, never.' "Do you lust?" and they say, "Not any more than the next person."

And when you come to sift it, you find [people] sheltering themselves under the general term sinner, not to make confession, but to evade it. Spurgeon (*Spurgeon at His Best*, 39) noted that we often hear things like, "We all sin; I'm a sinner just like everybody else." And that lessens the responsibility to confess. Spurgeon continued to advise: The next time I hear someone say, "We all sin," I may ask that person, what particular sin they've been committing just to remain a part of the human race?

5) Another enemy of proper contrition is the natural preference for dwelling on the trivial ("Business," financial reports) than on the eternal. It is safer to deal with superficial matters; so we usually do so. If we allow that natural tendency to prevail, then we rarely have to attend to specific sin.

---

[20] Charles Spurgeon, *At His Best*, 39.

6) Assumption of inherent goodness is a sworn-enemy of confession. If people continue to think that humanity is good, then surely sin is a passing fad.

No doubt, if we set our minds to it, we could come up with other reasons to minimize confession.

However, let me tell you about what we can learn about confession. One of the greatest books in Christian history was a Confession. Over the next several chapters, I hope to introduce you or remind you about some prominent biblical themes that I think we all need to hear. We may not have thought about these in a while, so it behooves us to do so.

In each chapter in our series, I want to introduce you to each topic by using one of the greatest selling books in Christian history. I'd like to bring to you several insights from these classics of devotional literature. Every family needs to be a little familiar with these. I hope to stimulate you to read the entire book, and your Church Library should be used more than ever.

One of the greatest classics among Christian literature is Augustine's *Confessions*. This great thinker, Augustine, wrote his testimony (as) in the form of Confessions. He told about how he came to know God by his personal confession.

Aurelius Augustine, the bishop of Hippo Regius in Roman North Africa, greatest of the Latin Fathers lived 354-430. His parents were Patricius (a convert) and Monica, a committed Christian who is more well-known. He received much of his higher education at Carthage (371-75). He showed definite signs of mental excellence, particularly mastering the writings of the earlier Greek philosophers. Even though he was raised by a godly mother, he permitted himself, according to his own testimony in the Confessions, nearly every fleshly passion possible at the time. He even went so far as to enter into an unofficial marriage (372) which lasted until 385 and produced a son, Adeodatus ("gift of God").[21]

At first, Augustine seemed infatuated with philosophy, which soon led him into a super-spiritual cult, the Manichees. The Manichees held that true spirituality was found in the realm of

[21] Source: *New International Dictionary of Christian History)*, 86-87.

ideas or spirituality. For nearly 10 years, Augustine was consumed with this intense spirituality, but eventually found that it was lacking in fiber. He floundered for some time as a teacher of rhetoric (375-376) and went to Rome in 383, and fell under the spell of the gifted and eloquent Ambrose, bishop of Milan. While at Milan, he was introduced to Christian teaching which ultimately liberated him from the cultic ideas of the Manichees. His conversion from worldliness came one day while he was reading Romans 13:13, 14 (late summer 386). This led Augustine to reject his earlier career plans and study this new found religion as much as he could. Shortly thereafter, he was baptized by Ambrose in 387.

Later, Augustine wrote against Manichaeism. While visiting Hippo, he was strong-armed into the priesthood (391); later, he founded a monastery there.

In time, he would be associated with a radical diagnosis of man and history (even church history). His book, *The Confessions* (c. 397-401) interpret his earlier years up to Monica's death in light of his sin. He left behind many commentaries and writings that are still worth the time of those who live centuries later.

One of them was *The City of God* (c. 413-27) began as a defense against the charges that Christianity was responsible for the fall of the Roman Empire in 410. The Romans, looking for a convenient scapegoat, did as many moderns do: blamed all their problems on those pesky Christians. Even though Christianity, per se, had done nothing to abet the internal collapse of the Roman empire, nonetheless, they were blamed for it. St. Augustine wanted to provide a defense against such allegations. To do so, he attempted to put together a comprehensive review of history to show the ongoing conflict of powers: the city of this world and the city of God.

The classic work which addresses these matters, *The City of God*, seeks to illustrate the rival strains characteristic of belief and unbelief throughout the history of mankind. For him, one city was organized around the prowess and pride of man, complete with its materialism, violence, unbelief, lust for domination, and oppression; on the other hand, the *civitatis dei* was characterized by a profound love for God, valuation of the eternal over the temporal, high ethical standards, and equitable treatment of neighbors. Augustine's *City of God* was an apology for the Christian Church and its ethical values. In answer to the secular critics who sought to blame the fall of the Roman Empire on Christian beliefs and practices, Augustine strove to demonstrate instead that the seeds of societal corruption lie in the very morals and concepts of pre-Christian Roman paganism. Augustine alleged that the Roman Empire did not spread because imitators found great justice and freedom in it; rather, it spread by sheer force of conquest. Augustine also placed the blame for societal decay in the eclipse of virtue in the Roman era: "the good old customs have been lost, and for so great an evil not only are we responsible but we should face judgment, like culprits fearing the penalty of death. By our own vices, not by chance, we have lost the republic, though we retain the name." Certainly, Christian virtues did not cause the collapse of the Roman Empire, but Christians were liable to the judgment awarded to a corporate entity that had lost its ethical compass.

Like most good theologians, his teachings attracted no small amount of controversy. "Against the Manichaeans he defended the goodness of creation, and he developed a rationale of faith as evoked by the impressive authority of the universal church and leading to understanding. He was also an early leader in teaching against the idea that humans were all basically good.

Why is confession so important?

It has two senses. *First*, confession means 'to speak the same word' = *homologeo*. The word in the Bible for "confession" means to say the same thing, or to consent. In regard to sin, this word most truly refers to a person's acknowledgment that God is/was correct and that we are wrong. To confess, therefore, means to agree with God. "We were wrong; You were right, O God" is the essence of confession. The great Baptist Minister, Charles Spurgeon said: "We know this is absolutely necessary for salvation. Unless there is a true and hearty confession of our sins to God, we have no promise that we

SUMMER READING: CHRISTIAN CLASSICS

shall find mercy through the blood of the Redeemer. "Whoever confesses their sins and forsakes them shall find mercy." But there is no promise in the Bible to the man who will not confess his sins. Yet, as at every point of Scripture there is a liability of being deceived, so more especially in the matter of confession of sin. There are many who make a confession, and . . . receive no blessing, because their confession does not have in it the marks [of legitimacy]."

It is also possible to utter an insincere or unlasting confession. Several characters in Scripture gave a verbal confession, but it was not sincere. Pharaoh in Exodus 9:27 uttered the words "I have sinned," but there was no true repentance. His words were like billowing clouds that dissipate following a storm. His confession was like thunder or lightning—gone after the tumult. His was like the atheist in a foxhole who is converted under fire, only to return to spiritual callousness when the attack is over; or like the sailor who prays during a storm at sea, only to pursue abject drunkenness when he is back on land. Or like the student unprepared for a major exam. It is possible to make an insincere confession. Have you?

Some make such confessions on a sickbed, or when in dire circumstances. Do not think that you can lie to God. You may be able to fool your peers, but not God. A rash vow becomes a lie to God if not kept. "It is no use to say, 'I have sinned,' merely under the influence of terror, and then to forget it afterwards." (Spurgeon).

Balaam, the double-minded, also confessed, "I have sinned." (Num. 22:34); Saul, too, uttered, "I have sinned" (1 Sam. 15:24)—but he was insincere; Achan confessed, "I have sinned" (Josh. 7:20); and even Judas (Mt. 27:4) admitted that he sinned. Mere verbalizing of one's sinfulness does not save.

So do not think that confession alone will save. Jesus said, "Not all who SAY 'Lord, Lord' enter the kingdom of heaven, but only those who do my Father's will."

Some people seem to have hearts made of putty (elastic). When they are in church, their hearts seem malleable even to the touch, but when they leave, they their hearts are equally impressionable by the ways of the world.

But do not forget this verse: "If you confess with your mouth,' Jesus is Lord,' and believe in your heart that God raised him from the dead, you will be saved. For it is with your heart that you believe and are justified, and it is with your mouth that you confess and are saved." (Rom. 10:9-10)

The *second* meaning of confession is to agree with a statement of faith. Some churches are rediscovering the value of standards of belief in an age that is skeptical about nearly everything. Fixed standards of truth are making a comeback. We have had a confession for some time, and it is useful.

Following the last 30 years of fitful flirtation with relativism, evangelicals are returning to the value of Confessions. One such group to arise is the Alliance of Confessing Evangelicals (sponsor of a great blog, Ref21). Among them were well known names like R. C. Sproul, Michael Horton, Al Mohler, and others (Lutherans, Baptists. Anglicans, Presbyterians, and dispensationalists).

They realized that evangelicals were losing the battle to modernity without some fixed forms of truth. In the face of the winds of modernity, we must have some anchors that do not change or fade. Confessions are an age-old way of expressing this.

Samuel Miller, long ago asked: "What is a church without a confession? She is like a ship without sails amidst a storm."

Why, as early as the NT, we even find remnants of early confessions in the following passages:

1 Timothy 6:12-13 refers to Jesus himself as making a good confession before Pilate. Likewise, Christians are commended for making their "good confession in the presence of many witnesses." Matthew teaches ("If you confess me before men . . . I will confess you before my father) to bring out public nature of faith. Real faith is confessed.

Romans 14:11 looks like an early confessional summary. It says, "It is written: As surely as I live, says the Lord, 'Every knee will bow before me and every tongue confess to God. . ." Those words are nearly identical to what is written in Philippians 2. The explanation is that these were part of a memorized early creed.

Philippians 2:11 may be a remnant of an early Christian creed, focusing on the incarnation and exaltation of Christ. It contains those words above that every knee will bow and every tongue confess that Jesus Christ is Lord.

1 Corinthians 12:3 says, "No one can say, 'Jesus is Lord,' except by the Holy Spirit. "Jesus is Lord" was apparently an early confession.

Hebrews 3:1 calls on Christians everywhere to "fix your thoughts on Jesus, the apostle and high priest whom we confess." Early Christians understood the value of public confessions.

The Bible speaks of this need **to have confessions and to practice confession**.

Proverbs 28:13 teaches: "He who conceals his sins does not prosper, but whoever confesses and renounces them finds mercy."

In the NT, 1 John 1:9 teaches, "If we confess our sins, he is faithful and just to forgive us all unrighteousness." This forgiveness of all sin—past, present, and future—is linked to our confession. Certainly God is the one who can do it and it does not depend on us. However, we are called to confess; that is our duty.

There is something vital about uniting our mouths with our hearts. God knew that this would be a real need. If belief is kept internal only, and never bubbles out of our mouths, it is hardly belief, or at least it is not very important. We do talk about those things that are real important to us. It is important for us to love Jesus enough to talk about him with our peers.

Jesus stressed this in Mt. 15: "Out of the abundance of the heart, the mouth speaks." Truly, our speech is an overflow from our mouths.

Spurgeon (*At His Best*, 38-39) says: "Imagine that some creditor has a debtor who owes him a thousand pounds. He calls him and says, 'I demand my money.' 'But,' says the other, 'I owe you nothing,' That man will be arrested and thrown into prison. However, the creditor says, 'I wish to deal mercifully with you. Make a frank confession, and I will forgive you all the debt.'

'Well,' says the man, 'I do acknowledge that I owe you 200 pounds.' 'No,' says he, 'that will not do.' 'Well sire, I confess I owe you 500 pounds,' and by degrees he comes to confess that he owes the thousand. Is there any merit in that confession? No, but yet you could see that no creditor would think of forgiving a debt which was not acknowledged. It is the least you can do to acknowledge your sin. And though there be no merit in the confession, yet, true to his promise, God will give you pardon through Christ."

He further added: "It is easy to commit sin, but hard to confess it. Man will transgress without a tempter. But even when urged by the most earnest pleader, he will not acknowledge his guilt." "It does not spoil your happiness to confess your sin. The unhappiness is in not making the confession."

Pride is a huge stumblingblock to confession. Pride comes in many forms.

Confession is also important at conversion. Perhaps you have "heard the story of the English king who was angry with the town-leaders of Calais, and declared that he would hang six of them. They [reported] to him with ropes about their necks, submitting to their doom. That is the way [you need to] come to Jesus. I accept my punishment, plead guilty, and beg for pardon. Put your rope upon your neck, confess that you deserve to die, and come to Jesus." (Spurgeon, *At His* Best, p. 39)

St. Augustine is a father in the faith that we could learn from. Confession has a valid role in the Christian life. If you have never confessed Christ publicly, then I wish you'd speak to me afterwards, or call a pastor or an elder this week, and I'll help you do that. Don't be one of those who cares more about what people think of you. Even if you are slightly embarrassed, that would be better than failing to confess Christ.

Augustine died as Roman Africa succumbed to the Vandals besieging Hippo. His friend Possidius, bishop of Calama, compiled a Life and a catalogue of his works. One of the last was the *Revisions* (*Retractationes*, 426-27), in which Augustine listed his writings, correcting and defending himself at points. Confession, there!

Confession is also valuable for ongoing growth. When we know Christ as forgiver, we ought not be too afraid to confess. In this week to come, I challenge you to find one instance in which you can confess your sin. Just one. Why, if you can't do that, you must be among the greatest of Christians. Then next week, add your quota to two. Our confession may even grow. This is a habit that goes against the grain, but we must learn it.

Also, study this great confession: The Prodigal in Luke 15:18 is a good model. After he had squandered his father's wealth, after he'd floundered in an immoral pig-sty, note how confession is a coming to one's senses. It implies that when we put down our stubborn pride, we can admit that God is right. "When he came to his senses, he said, 'How many of my father's hired men have food to spare, and here I am starving to death? . . . I am no longer worthy to be called your son. . .'" That's what true confession is like. We admit that we are not worthy, we are not always correct; we have failed. *It is more sensible to confess when we have sinned than it is to persist.* No doubt, some of you have come to worship loaded with some grievous sin. You need to confess it and leave it behind. Stop disputing with God; stop justifying yourself, and admit to God that in that specific area, you are not worthy. Prodigals come home.

If you do, the loving father is waiting; he takes the initiative and readily receives back those who sin and repent.

Earlier in Luke, a Woman's confession is seen in Luke 7:44 ff. In this case, she humbled herself and washed the Lord's feet with her hair and tears. She loved Jesus enough that she gave up her pride. She loved him so much as is seen in her so great act of devotion. Immediately afterwards, the Pharisees dispute Jesus in this. He tells a short parable about a person who had been forgiven a huge debt.

Comparably speaking, the one who has been forgiven greater amounts tends to love in greater degree. Jesus saw that in this woman. He forgave all her sins (47) and stated that she had great love. The climax is our Lord's saying: "He who loves much is forgiven much. But he who has been forgiven little loves little." Could it be that you think you have only been forgiven a little? If your love for the Lord seems waning, it may be related to your blindness, your failure to see how much Jesus has forgiven. Can you see how much he has forgiven you for? Can't you say with Paul, "I am the chief of sinners"? If so, we love much in the realization of forgiveness. Confession is related to our love for the Lord.

Whenever we confess, we show that God is Lord and we are servants. Every time we confess a sin that puts our life in proper perspective. That is one of the reasons why we need to renew this practice.

One of Augustine's disciples centuries later was Charles Spurgeon: "Sin confessed with tears, sin which causes the very heart to bleed—killing sin, damning sin—this is the kind of sin for which Jesus died. Sham sinners may be content with a sham Savior, but our Lord Jesus is the real Savior who did really die, and died for real sin. Oh, how this ought to comfort you who are sadly bearing the pressing burden of an abominable life! (*Spurgeon At His Best*, 39)

There is also a persistent need for balance in this area.

Augustine, though he is dead, still confesses.

Chapter 4

Luther's *Bondage of the Will*

John 8:31-37; Rom. 6:12-23

Twentieth century German martyr Dietrich Bonhoeffer said: "Luther's return from the cloister to the world was the worst blow the world had suffered since the days of early Christianity." (*Cost of Discipleship*, 51)

Luther's greatness can be gauged from the fact that during the four-hundred-fifty years since his death, more books have been written about him than about any other figure in history, except Jesus of Nazareth.

A sketch of his life is appended to the end of this chapter. Of course, most people are aware of his posting of the Ninety-Five Theses on October 31, 1517. In April of 1521 Luther stood before the emperor and other rulers at the Diet of Worms, and declined to recant in the famous words that are now associated with him: "Unless my conscience is held captive by the words of Scripture, I can do no other. Here I stand, God Help me; I can do no other."

In 1525, he wrote a religious work that would prove to be one of the most significant religious books of all time. In that work, Luther took on one of the giants of the day, Erasmus and his *Diatribe on Free Will* (1524). In Luther's answer, *The Bondage of the Will* (1525), he affirmed that man cannot will to turn to God or play any part in the process leading to his own salvation. That's what I want to discuss in this chapter.

For much of our consideration today, it will help if we first of all note that Luther's work concentrated on the Bondage—*not the Temporary Insanity*—of the Will. Luther, following the biblical teachings, did not think that the ability of man—no matter how much willpower it had—could do as God wanted. He taught that the will or capability of man was in chains; it was bound. Radically contrary to modern notions, the Bible does not suggest that we are free to do anything or everything we would like to. Here's how Luther put it: "The very name, Free-will, was odious to all the Fathers. I, for my part, admit that God gave to mankind a free-will, but the question is, whether this same freedom be in our power and strength, or not. We [have] a subverted, perverse, fickle, and wavering will, for it is only God that works in us, . . . for we are not able to do any-thing that is good in divine matters."[22]

We frequently hear people talk about willpower and pulling oneself up by his bootstraps. But according to the Bible that rhetoric overestimates human potential; it is quite inflated. Let's compare that man-made myth with God's Word.

Early in the Scriptural narratives, we find that God's opinion of human ability is roughly as follows:

- Gen. 6:5: God saw that every inclination of the thoughts of his heart were only evil all the time."
- After the flood, Gen. 8:21 reiterates: "Never again will I curse the ground because of man, even though every inclination of his heart is evil from childhood."
- Ps. 51:5 affirms, "Surely I was sinful at birth, sinful from the time my mother conceived me."
- Jer. 17:9 teaches, "The heart is deceitful above all things; who can cure?"

---

[22] *The Table Talk of Martin Luther* (Baker, 1995), 159-160.

The OT depicts sinners as those who may occasionally do the moral thing. But on balance, they have an ability-level that is enchained. The bondage of the will is taught in the OT. Martin Luther did not make it up. Even though at the time of the Renaissance, scholars had a more optimistic view of human nature, Luther was right to oppose the freedom of the will as an unbiblical notion.

This view of the enchained will hardly changes at the beginning of the NT. Listen to a few of Jesus' own teachings.

In **John 6**, he told a group that they could not come to him on their own or even if they liked. Our Savior taught the bondage of the will when he said, "No man can come unto me, unless the Father who sent me draws him." (Jn. 6:44). A person was not free, according to Jesus, to volunteer to come to him. A person with an enchained will had first to be drawn by Jesus' Father.

Earlier, he had told Nicodemus that it was impossible for him to do as God wanted apart from the Holy Spirit. Nicodemus would first have to be born again, changed in nature. The human will is not as free as we'd like to think.

In **John 8:32-36**, Jesus spoke to the Jews and told them that if they held to his teaching they could be his disciples and know the truth. Knowledge of that truth would set them free. They, however, took umbrage at that and were insulted. They screamed back at Jesus, with veins popping out of their necks: "We ARE Abraham's descend-ants and have never been slaves of anyone. How can you say that we shall be set free?" They had the nerve to claim that they had never been enslaved, despite the facts of Egypt, Babylonia, Rome, etc. The Jews were proud not only of their heritage, but also of their ability. They did not enjoy someone telling them that they needed some liberation.

Jesus answered: "I tell you the truth, everyone who sins is a slave to sin." **Ouch**. That made them furious. Did Jesus know that would make him furious? Only if he was omniscient. And he was! Jesus held to the view that all people—not merely Jews—were slaves to one principle or another. Those who were not born again were slaves to sin. And that slave had no permanent place in the home. He was not a son. Jesus knew exactly what he was saying; so did the Jews. And so did Luther later. The human will is born enslaved. It just is. It cannot soar without restriction.

The human will cannot do anything in the world it would like to. It cannot do all things. It cannot even do good apart from the Holy Spirit in us. In John 15, Jesus stated that "apart from me you can do nothing." Not even the strongest of human wills can do what it wants apart from Christ.

Rom. 6 affirms the same teaching later in the NT. These verses teach us that we're all slaves: You are slaves to the one you obey. This is not so much theory as practice.

A) Non-Christians

According to Rom. 6:16, a non-Christian does not have near the freedom he may think. A Non-Christian is actually a slave to sin, which leads to death. Rather than having unrestricted freedom to choose anything, the non-Christian, even if he does not know it, serves sin, culminating in death. It the irrational kind of idiocy inbred by sin that is observed in watching a person in bondage, in horrible crippling slavery. It is a slavery of the cruelest type . . . a slavery that allows no real freedom, no true personhood, one which *reduces a man or woman to a machine-slave to sin.* Non-Christians are in these kinds of chains—and they don't even know it. They are slaves to the cruelest of taskmasters, one who always pays out death.

Don't be confused and think non-Christians are free. You see the worst kind of bondage in sexual sin, whose lust will not rest, and whose master drives the body of that sinner, until some kind of disaster or disease leads to death. That will is bound, chained.

* The compulsive, unrestrained person with lethal ambition is bound by that will.
* The person who hates by nature is not free to love.
* It is no excuse, but the person who repeatedly commits adultery or theft or slander exhibits the bondage of the will.

To use the military metaphor from Romans 6: Sin is the sovereign commander who conscripts his subjects into the military. He issues the arms of unrighteousness to these loyal sin-soldiers to use in service of their master. And when it is over, he gives them soldier's salary, in this case . . . death.

The same dynamic is true for other types of sin, as well. It is not merely those visible or ugly sins that obey this rule of slavery. But those nearly-invisible sins do this, as well. Sin yields slavery not freedom. And when you sin, it is not an act of freedom, but one of slavery to follow the devil.

B) Christians are also bound by the human will, except for what the Holy Spirit does. Vss. 17-18

Christians also are slaves, but the mirror opposite of the slave to sin. Thanks be to God, that although we are slaves, it is a blessed bondage, a routine that brings true freedom, and in the way that the world least expects it. We who once were slaves to sin, according to v. 17 now obey the form of teaching "from the heart." It is not a mere formalism that drives us, but a willing and consecrated desire to wholeheartedly obey God from the heart. When God's commands become clear from Scripture, or from the preaching of the Word, do you rush to obey from the heart? Is it your desire to do what God wants you to, or do you grouse about it? Find ways to avoid it?

Now that we're Christians, we have a new nature. And, just as before "Nature determines Will." Now that we're new slaves, transferred from one Master to another, we have becomes "slaves to righteousness" (v. 18). That is what we now serve . . . right living. You may even want to think of it *in the language of addiction. We, who are slaves to righteousness, are hooked on living* as God wants us, and we serve him. But, make no mistake about it, we are slaves. We all are. The eternal difference is that the one is a slavery which leads to death, while the other leads to eternal life.

As Paul teaches, when you were slaves to sin, you not only did not, and could not choose righteousness, you were "Free from the control of righteousness" (V. 20). And the crop you reaped from that was shame, death, and sin.

Has sin dominion over you? I did not say, 'Do you sin?' for 'if we say we have no sin, we deceive ourselves and the truth is not in us' (1 Jn. 1:8). But I ask, 'Has sin dominion over you'?"

Not too long ago, our church spent several Sundays in Romans 7. That classic chapter has been a comfort to many, but also a challenge to the idea of the perfectibility of the human will.

Before we come to Christ, that nature from which we cannot escape dominates us. It controls us. It handicaps us, severely restricts our options, does not allow free choice. It controls us. The pre-Christian is **a controlled person**, a *person managed by sin*, a slave to sin.

The Pre-Christian person is also portrayed as having sinful passions aroused. It was with passion alright, with lustful and enthusiastic zest that we engaged in sinful acts. *Not only was it our nature, but it was also our will*, and our passions were aroused by sin. This soon led to bodily manifestation. The sin we engage in, never remains purely in our minds. It always, unless crucified, finds a way to be acted out. It becomes bodily manifested. Prior to being a Christian, we were people who were known by sinful passions.

In Romans 7, we saw Paul, one of the greatest Christians, struggling with sin. From that, we learn both of the persistent presence of sin in the life of the believer, as well as the victory which God ultimately gives. Note what is clear from the text.

Paul viewed himself as if he was a slave, "sold into slavery." He honestly assesses his sinfulness, and begins to realize that he is not as powerful as he would like to be. He cannot conquer all his sin, in his own strength. In fact, he feels like one who is not in control, but one who is a slave, an involuntary servant to sin. Even the most mature Christians still sin, and at times feel as if they are so spiritually impotent, as to be slaves of sin, sold into bondage.

Paul thought he was doing pretty well until he considered the law and its true spotlight on the sinner's soul (9-10).

If you ever think you've satisfied the law, go back and think again, for you've misunderstood it. The law is given by God, precisely to convict us. God wants us convicted. That is how he works with us—Yes even mature Christians, like Paul. It is only when we're convicted, that we begin to listen to God; only in that brokenness that we forsake our self-sufficiency. Conviction shows us our need.

That's exactly what happened to Paul, numerous times. Back in Romans 7:8, he has in mind a time of conviction, specifically over coveting, and he relates in that episode, how the more he looked at coveting, the more he saw his sin. Sin, seemed to be magnified, when under the lens of the law. Indeed, maybe the Law is a magnifying glass for sin, to push us to our knees and to Christ. As Paul says it, "Sin seized the opportunity afforded by the commandment" and produced in me every kind (Or more) of covetous desire. As Paul became aware of the law's true and internal scope, it showed how truly sinful he was. That is why we must preach the law: to seek that same effect in others' lives. Especially among mature Christians, like Paul.

Paul is quick to admit that he was at a loss to understand this phenomena. You probably are, too. It does seem a bit mystifying to watch ourselves sin, especially when we know how much God has done for us. Yet, the presence of sin is too pervasive to deny. For Paul, "What I want to do, I do not do, but what I hate (strong term = loathe) to do" (v. 15). Yes, at times Christians do the exact opposite of what they want to do. That is the 'bondage of the will', as Luther called it.

Can you believe the vaunted apostle Paul said this? I mean, can it possibly be true that "Nothing good lives in me, that is, in my sinful nature? Is that your own view of your human ability and potential? Over time, *I have become a thorough disciple of Paul in this regard.* I've learned that "there is no good dwelling in me." Now that's not so much a dreary view of mankind as it is an honest admission that if anything works out good, it is a by-product of God's handiwork. All the credit for mistakes and sins rests with me. If "Nothing good lives in me," then the only possible source of good, is God.

If you have not already come to this point in your Christian life, I urge you to join the "Chief of Sinners" club and begin to be realistic.

We find that there is something about this struggle with sin. We grow through these episodes and are kept humble by God, who sustains us - even through imperfection.

Other NT scriptures teach a similar "Struggle with Sin"

Philippians 3 portrays Paul as struggling with the past. He resolves to leave the past behind as press onward toward the future. If there had been no struggle, he would not need to make this new resolve.

2 Corinthians 5 also depicts for us, the struggle as long as we are "at home in the body." The Christian's real desire is to be "away with the Lord," free from sin. It is precisely this ongoing struggle with sin that gives our final liberation such meaning.

Ephesians 6 also speaks of the hand-to-hand wrestling, kind of struggle, in which we resist the prince of darkness and seek to avoid his conquest over us. The Bible makes it clear that the ongoing struggle in the Christian life, is one to expect, and unfortunately to get to know, until we are finally freed from it. That Bondage dogs us all our days.

Paul recognizes that he is the chief of sinners. "I am unspiritual, sold as a slave to sin." *True humility is a result of knowing the Bondage of the Will.*

The writer of Romans 7 exhibits the attributes of a Christian. Even his will was severely limited. The passage proves the bondage of the will, not only BEFORE conversion, but AFTER conversion. *We are always slaves.* It is just a question of Whom we serve.

Let me briefly introduce you to the four fold state of man. This concept appears to be original with St. Augustine, but so many later theologians have spoken of it, that it is difficult to tell who made this famous. But I want to share with you what is called "The Four-fold State of Man." It is a clever description of the history of the human will. For all who think willpower is a good thing, listen to this.

(1) **Able not to sin.** (*posse non peccare*)

When Adam was first created, he had the freedom of the will not to do sin; yet that condition was changeable as the Fall obviously illustrates. At first, Adam obeyed God perfectly and did as God wanted. Adam's will was in line with God's. He had no sin-disposition, nor bias. There was no compulsion of the will to sin. Adam was free of bondage of the will until he sinned. Then that changed everything.

(2) **Not able not to sin**. (*non posse non peccare*)
Following the Fall, the human will has been bound and incapable of avoiding sin. Even the best of us sins. No one escapes the magnetic pull of sin. The human will is unable not to sin. We are born with this tendency which leads to actual transgressions and our will is far from uniformly or inherently good.

(3) **Able to sin, or resist by God's Spirit**. (*posse peccare*)
A change for the better does, however, occurs at conversion. When we are recreated after the image of Christ, we are then enabled to follow God. Although we do still sin, we are given new capabilities. Whereas once the will could never do the right thing, now through the power of Christ, we can obey God. We are no longer slaves to unrighteousness. We may be slaves to God and serve him. We are able to sin, but do not always do so, thanks to sanctification.

(4)   **Not able to sin**. (*non posse peccare*)
In the glorified state, we will be free from temptation to sin, or actual commitment of sin. We will be delivered from sin, and our wills will never choose nor fall into sin. We will not be able to sin. It will be impossible, as our nature and wills are healed and removed from the curse of sin. We will never fall away from God, nor choose to go against him. We will have the will to obey him as he ought.

Several other metaphors are employed:
  * "captive unlocked"

* Acts 8:23—Simon Magus is "full of bitterness and captive to sin."
* 2 Tim. 2:26 shows that it is the devil's desire to "take [people] captive to do his will."
* Is 61:1 speaks of how the Sovereign Lord liberates the captives and releases convicts from the darkness of prison.

John Gerstner, the theological mentor to R. C. Sproul, summarized much theology in this: "Man is either sick, or weak, or dead." If he is sick, he needs remediation or therapy. If he is weak, he needs training or exercise. But if he is dead, he needs resurrection—nothing less will do.

This teaching had a wide impact on Western Civilization Many of our laws and penalties are based on this view of the human will. There are numerous implications of view.

We live in an age that is dogmatically committed to thinking of men and women as free, unhindered, and able to provide for themselves. That is a fantasy, and any social program or plan for individual reform that is based on that will fail.

Even secular groups that are successful agree with Luther on the bondage of the will. AA, for example, demands that the first step for recovery is a recognition that one cannot solve his own problems by himself. If an organization that is not explicitly Christian has this figured out, shame on the church if we have an inferior understanding of this key teaching. Our wills are bound.

Sometimes, in the process of sanctification, we have to admit that we are unable by the force of will to do all things we should; no matter how hard we try, we will fail at times.

As much as anything else, conversion illustrates the bondage of the will and the liberation of the gospel. The Bible describes conversion as an act performed by God. It is too mighty for us to execute. We cannot do it without him. In conversion, he takes a deadened sinner with a heart harder than stone, and a will that is in chains, and God awakens the dead, melts the heart of stone—transforming it into a supple obedient heart—and gives the sinner a new will. Then and only then can the person call out to God, or express love to him.

That is how we're made new, by God's powerful Spirit at work!

By this (bad news) teaching, Luther elevated the virtue of conversion (good news). Conversion "is the standing miracle of the church." (*Spurgeon at his Best*, p. 42). "Conversion is of absolute importance. It is the hinge of the gospel. . . . It is a physical impossibility that a swine should deliver a lecture on astronomy. Every man will clearly perceive that it must be impossible that a snail should build a city. And there is just as much impossibility [in light of the bondage of the will] that a sinner, unmended should enjoy heaven."

Other applications include:

The first step in repentance is admitting weakness. Overconfidence in terms of human ability is a serious mistake.

Luther admitted: "I have often been resolved to live uprightly, and to lead a true godly life, and to set everything aside that would hinder this, but it was far from being put in execution; even as it was with Peter, when he swore he would lay down his life for Christ. I will not lie or dissemble before my God, but will freely confess, I am not able to effect that good which I intend, but await the happy hour when God shall be pleased to meet me with his grace." (*The Table Talk of Martin Luther*, Baker, 1995, 160)

Why don't you begin this new week with that confession of human ability? And walk before the Lord in the coming days aware that your will is not as strong as humanists say, and is weak—only able to please the Lord if his strong grace conquers, fills, and reshapes your will. Then you will find freedom.

Appendix: Bio Sketch from the *New International Dictionary of the Christian Church*.

Born in Eisleben, Luther (1483-1546) was educated in Mansfield, and came under the influence of the Brethren of the Common Life while in Magdeburg. He enrolled at the Univ. of Leipzig in 1501, and received his M.A. in 1505. In July of that year Luther became an Augustinian monk in Erfurt, due to a vow made in "a moment of terror," when thrown to the ground by a bolt of lightning during a thunderstorm. He studied in the monastery and was ordained priest in 1507.

1508 Luther was transferred to the University of Wittenberg, where he later earned the doctor of theology degree in 1512. During these years he lectured on moral theology, the *Sentences* of Peter Lombard, and the Bible. Between November 1510 and March 1511 he was on a journey to Rome as a companion of a fellow friar on business for his order. With the doctor's degree Luther received the permanent appointment to the chair of *lectura in Biblia* at Wittenberg.

During these years before he became a doctor of theology, Luther was wrestling with the problem of his personal salvation. While in the monastery and as friar in Wittenberg he assiduously performed the required tasks and offices, frequently went to confession, and fulfilled the imposed penances. His "Tower Experience," the full realization of the meaning of justification by grace alone, likely occurred in 1514. The continued study of Scripture, the influence of Augustine, the writings of John Tauler and other mystics, and the advice of his superior Johann Staupitz were determinative probably in that order in clarifying his thoughts and convictions; yet no one date or moment can be certain. By 1518, his theology of the Cross was thoroughly Pauline, and Luther championed *sola fide* (faith alone), *sola gratia* (grace alone), *sola Scriptura* (the Bible alone).

In his writings between 1516 and 1518 Luther evidences his Augustinianism. In *Two Kinds of Righteousness* (1518), Luther clearly speaks of Christ and his work from his birth to his death and resurrection as constituting the righteousness of believers. These thoughts are present in his lectures on the Psalms and on Hebrews (1518). By this time Luther had issued his famous protest against the scandals of the indulgence traffic, the Ninety-Five Theses of 31 October 1517. The most noteworthy of these is number 62: "The true treasure of the church is the most holy Gospel of the glory and grace of God." His *Explanations of the Ninety-Five Theses* (1518) states, "The merits of Christ perform an alien work." The alien righteousness is the righteousness which he defines in his sermon on the *Two Kinds of Righteousness* as "the righteousness of another, instilled from without, the righteousness of Christ by which He justifies through faith."

The year 1520 marked the appearance of some of Luther's most important reformatory writings. The following essential doctrines were enunciated in some of these early writings:

- Faith is implemented in the life of the believer: *Treatise on Good Works* (May 1520).
- Every Christian is a priest: *Sermon on the Mass* (April 1520).
- The pope was branded "the real Anti-Christ of whom all the Scripture speaks." *On The Papcy at Rome* (June 1520).
- Luther disallowed the authority of the pope over temporal rulers, denied that the pope was the final interpreter of Scripture, decried the corruption of the Curia, affirmed again the universal priesthood of the believers, and spelled out a program of the church reforms: *The Address to the German Nobility* (August 1520).
- He reduced the number of sacraments from seven to two: *Concerning the Babylonian Captivity of the Church* (October 1520).

He defended two propositions: "A Christian is a perfectly free lord of all, subject to none. A Christian is a perfectly dutiful servant of all, subject to all.": *The Freedom of a Christian.*

Chapter 5

Calvin and *Institutional Christianity*

1 Timothy 1:18-19, 4:11-16

If someone wants to really assassinate your Christian character, they may call you a Calvinist. Sometimes it seems to me that the deepest, darkest theological cuss word is: Calvinist. By that, usually a person is calling you dogmatic, predestinarian, anti-free-will, and may even accuse you of wanting to burn others at stake. As usual, such stereotypes hardly fit.

Often the reputation of John Calvin (1509-1564) is besmirched by his secular and unsympathetic critics with charges that he is rationalistic and impassionately theoretical. One earlier critic accused him of being rationalistic prior to rationalism and Cartesian even before Descartes Calvin is consistently portrayed by many modern critics as if he were a twentieth century logical positivist—possessed only by the objective facts, the mechanistic urge and unappreciative of any emotional or practical considerations. Calvin is represented by some to be the cold theologian in the laboratory—removed from practicality, oblivious to his own and others' humanity, and impervious to feeling. He is consequently maligned by much of twentieth century Christendom with the unpardonable sins of rationality, logicality, and consistency. To a large degree, of course, much of this improper caricature (for it truly is a caricature) is promulgated by those who, at base, disagree not with Calvin's methodology, but the conclusions of his theology.

Our church is a Calvinistic one; the one I was raised in was not. Some people, despite our record, words, and deeds, continue to think that we are evil if we believe in the very biblical doctrine of election.

It might help you to know a little about Calvin[23] and his *Institutes*. This is a kind of "institutional" religion that will benefit you.

Little is known about Calvin's mother Jeanne la France of Cambrai (due to her early death), and his father was a dominant presence in his early life and education. He was the middle son in a family with five children—three sons and two daughters—born on July 10, 1509 in Noyon, a small town about an hour northeast of Paris. His father, Gerard, was an administrative assistant in the nearby cathedral complex, and his mother died when Calvin was only five.[24] His first biographer, his friend and colleague, Professor Theodore Beza, later described him as "of middle stature, sallow features, and whose piercing eye and animated looks announced a mind of no common sagacity."[25]

Calvin received a classical education in Paris, Orleans, Bourges, Basle. He was exposed to the thought of Erasmus, Le Fevre, Wolmar, and Francois Rabelais, a veritable *Who's Who* of Western European education for his day. Calvin would later complete the equivalent of a master's degree in Paris in an education that ranked with or surpassed Cambridge or Oxford at the time. A free market of new ideas and Protestantism (originally thought of as "Lutheranism") surged in Paris while Calvin was a student.

---

[23] The biographical sketch below is taken in part from my *The Legacy of John Calvin* (Phillipsburg, NJ: Presbyterian and Reformed, 2008).

[24] William J. Bouwsma, *John Calvin: A Sixteenth-Century Portrait* (New York: Oxford University Press, 1988), 9.

[25] Cited in See J. H. Merle D'Aubigne, *The History of the Reformation of the Sixteenth Century* (New York: American Tract Society, 1848), vol. 3, 474. See Theodore Beza, *Life of John Calvin* (contained in John Calvin, *Tracts and Treatises on the Reformation of the Church* [Grand Rapids, MI: Eerdmans, 1958]), vol. 1.

His first published work, a commentary on Seneca's *De Clementia* (1532), affirmed the radical notion that "[T]he prince is not above the laws, but the laws above the prince."[26] Later, his published works would concentrate on a wide array of theological subjects.

If it had been left up to his wishes, John Calvin would have continued to pursue a comfortable academic career. He did not intend either to serve as a pastor or to work in Geneva, but God had other plans for him.

Calvin's only autobiographical account of his spiritual conversion appears in the 1557 Preface to his *Commentary on Psalms*.[27] He did not wear his conversion on his sleeve but took many opportunities to practice what he preached. From Calvin's own testimony, he rarely saw himself as breaking new ground, and he described the Book of Psalms as "An Anatomy of all the parts of the Soul." No sterile scholastic, as often maligned, he claimed that "there is not an emotion of which any one can be conscious that is not here [in the Psalms] represented as in a mirror." All the "lurking places" of the heart were illumined in these devotional poems.

After this "sudden conversion," the Parisian student found himself "inflamed with an intense desire," and he fervently pursued Protestant teachings. After a year of diligent study (so intense perhaps because Protestantism was new and also because Calvin studied under some of the finest teachers in the pristine movement), he was surprised that numerous people began to treat him like an expert on these matters. He humbly viewed himself as unpolished, bashful, retiring, and preferring seclusion. Yet, like the author of the Psalms, he sensed that he was inevitably being thrust into the role of a public leader. Instead of successfully living in scholarly quiescence, all his retreats became public debating

---

[26] Harro Hopfl, *The Christian Polity of John Calvin* (Cambridge: Cambridge University Press, 1982), 16.

[27] All citations from Calvin's self-testimony about his spiritual conversion are taken from *Calvin's Commentaries*, vol. 4 (rpr. Grand Rapid: Baker Book House, 1979).

forums. He wrote: "In short, while my one great object was to live in seclusion without being known, God so led me about through different turnings and changes that he never permitted me to rest in any place, until in spite of my natural disposition, he brought me forth to public notice."

Calvin wanted to avoid the fray, nevertheless. His own spiritual pilgrimage indicates that he resolved to devote himself to quiet scholarly obscurity, until William Farel detained him in Geneva, "not so much by counsel and exhortation as by a dreadful imprecation, which I felt to be as if God had from heaven laid his mighty hand upon me to arrest me." The myths about Farel's imprecation are numerous. Even though the exact words are lost, it is clear that Farel applied some fiery threats to Calvin's conscience.

He published his first edition of *The Institutes of the Christian Religion* in 1536 and settled in Geneva for two years as a lecturer in Scripture. After a short time, however, he was exiled to Strasbourg, where he would pastor other refugees, learn from other leading reformers, and find a wife (Idelette de Bure). He returned to Geneva in 1541 with trepidation, but the Lord blessed his ministry there until his death in 1564. When he died, the city mourned.

When Calvin returned to St. Pierre Cathedral in 1541, he unceremoniously but symbolically resumed his pulpit activity by expounding the Scriptures at the exact verse where he left off prior to his exile. Contrary to the stereotype that Calvin was a dry or uninteresting pedant, his sermons actually attracted large and consistent audiences. By the mid-1550s, one eyewitness reported that most Genevans, "even the hypocrites," heard these Calvinistic sermons.[28] During most of Calvin's tenure, sermons were preached daily from all four of Geneva's churches. Stressing simplicity and clarity, Calvin's preaching was ideally designed to persuade the masses and to shape their expectations. His preaching was pervasive, and one of Theodore Beza's 1561 letters to William Farel claimed that over one thousand people heard Calvin's

[28] E. William Monter, *Calvin's Geneva*, 99.

lectures on a daily basis—a considerable mass communication accomplishment for the day.[29] Calvin's sermons eventually yielded 44 volumes in manuscript form—a prolific achievement considering Calvin had so many other duties.

During his final residence in Geneva, Calvin regularly preached expositions in the three Sunday services. By 1549, these messages were so popular that they were increased to daily expositions. Calvin's rotation allowed him to preach twice on Sunday and every day in alternating weeks. On average, Calvin thus prepared 20 sermons per month, normally drawing on New Testament texts on Sunday mornings, Old Testament texts during the week, and the Psalms on Sunday afternoons. His fertile mind could not be limited only to writing. Calvin preached 200 sermons on Deuteronomy, 159 on Job, 110 on 1 Corinthians, and 43 on Galatians—intellectual achievements in their own right. By these free and spirited orations, the common man was enlightened and equipped to carry the ideas of reform for a long time. Optimizing one medium would only inspire him to employ other means of mass communication as well.

His pioneering work to establish the Academy in Geneva also ensured that his ideas would survive more than in his own generation. Calvin further succeeded in educating the masses, as well as in training generations of pastors and civic leaders from his Academy. Both his school and its students would perpetuate the notions expounded in his sermons and writings. By Calvin's death in 1564, there were 1,200 students in the college and 300 in the seminary.

The Idea of Institutes

This 1559 work (the final edition), the most systematic of Calvin's works, is allegedly the work with the least *pathos*. However, if his practicality is emitted in his most theoretical work, then certainly coupled with his other practical and pastoral contributions, Calvin should be reassessed as an eminently practical theologian. *The Institutes* rather than being a cold systematic theology textbook, is a

---

[29] See Henry Martyn Baird, *Theodore Beza* (1899), 200.

book written during the Reformation *by* a practical Christian, *about* practical Christianity, *for* practical Christians (much like the claim of our constitution's motto "of the people, by the people, for the people"). Your spiritual life might benefit if you become acquainted with the practical Calvin.

The practical nature of this theological presentation can be observed from the following.

First it should be remembered that in the original edition of *The Institutes of the Christian Religion* (1536) there were only six chapters. Of the first four chapters, three of those were catechetical. The first chapter was on "Law," an exposition of the moral law or the Ten Commandments. The third chapter was an elaborate exposition of the Lord's Prayer, while the fourth chapter of the original edition was an explanation of the Protestant view of the Sacraments. Hence 75% of the earliest chapters in this first impression deal with material that is practical and basic for every Christian. These first four chapters are not filled with philosophical prolegomena, intricate definitions, nor theoretical ideals. Surprisingly they are written much like Luther's Catechism (It is interesting to ask why Luther does not equally share the same theological character assassination that Calvin does.), as practical instruction for practical Reformation Christians.

Thus, the original work was far from the ivory towers of academia; it was forged in the fires of practical Reformation Christianity. Calvin intended for this work to be a basic primer on elementary subjects germane to every Christian's life such as obedience to the Commandments, how to pray, faith itself, and the benefits of the Sacraments. It is important to note that Calvin did not begin his work with any categories drafted from philosophy, science, or theology. Instead he writes a practical treatise much like a catechism. In further revisions, to stress practicality and familiarity, he even organized the Institutes around the major *loci* of the Apostles Creed. Any expansions of the first edition should be interpreted in harmony with the authorial intent, unless explicitly or implicitly denied.

Second, it should be noted that Calvin's own self-understanding of his work, as enunciated in his own preface, is overtly practical. In his address to King Francis I he proffers an apologetic for Protestant Christianity. What could be, by the very nature of the case, more practical than the defense of a persecuted faith? Certainly such an apologetic endeavor, to a nonsympathizer, would not lead the reader to truncated notions and intricate theological matrixes. Rather, Calvin is practical. In the preface to the reader in the 1559 edition, Calvin's last will and testament within *The Institutes*, he re-affirms that he wrote as a theologian of the church of God when he speaks of his "effort to carry out this task for God's church."[30] He states the animating purpose of the final edition in these practical words: "God has filled my mind with zeal to spread his kingdom and to further the public good."[31] This is hardly an impractical purpose. Calvin further continues to state four reasons why he is finalizing this edition:[32]

(1) "I have had no other purpose than to benefit the church by maintaining the pure doctrine of godliness."

(2) To squelch the "rumor . . . spread abroad of my defection to the papacy."

(3) "To prepare and instruct candidates in sacred theology for the reading of the divine Word."

(4) To lay down a manifesto for his forthcoming and published commentaries so that he will "have no need to undertake long doctrinal discussions and to digress. . . ." in future writings.

Thirdly, the emphasis on the Holy Spirit's role in faith (paragraphs 33-36 & 39) is integral to Calvin's teaching. Again, even Calvin's theology of Faith is not scholastic. It is not the scholastic who writes, "For the Word of God is not received by faith if it flits about in the top of the brain, but when it takes root in the depth of the heart that it may be an invincible defense to withstand and drive off all the stratagems of temptation." (3:2-36)

In his demarcation of faith from hope, he says:

---

[30] John Calvin, *The Institutes of the Christian Religion*, J. T. McNeill, ed. (Philadelphia: Westminster, 1960), 3.

[31] Ibid., 4.

[32] Ibid., 4-5.

Accordingly, in brief, hope is nothing else than the expectation of those things which faith has believed to have been truly promised by God. Thus, faith believes God to be true, hope awaits the time when his truth shall be manifested; faith believes that he is our Father, hope anticipates that he will ever show himself to be a Father toward us; faith believes that eternal life has been given to us, hope anticipates that it will sometime be revealed; faith is the foundation upon which hope rests, hope nourishes and sustains faith. For as no one except him who already believes His promises can look for anything from God, so again the weakness of our faith must be sustained and nourished by patient hope and expectation, lest it fail and grow faint. (3:2-42)

What conference preacher could speak more clearly, more comprehensibly, or more forcefully to the average Christian than Calvin does in these words?

Calvin is also spoken of as the Theologian of the Holy Spirit. While you may not hear that very often, it is fair, especially in light of how many references he has to the work of the Holy Spirit. In contrast to the heavily-corseted Medieval theology before him, Calvin knew and spoke of the work of the Spirit more than most theologians of this time.

His institutes helped to reform both the church and the state. The teachings contained did not stoke the fires of chaos, nor was Calvin an anarchist. He believed that both the law of God as well as the precepts of the NT provided ample guidance for nations and for individuals. Yes his thought was rigorous, but to support the needed structure for a blossoming culture, such scaffolding was essential.

A few exemplary quotes may further tantalize us.

For it is a doctrine not of the tongue but of life . . . it is received when it possess the whole soul and finds a seat and resting place in the inmost affection of the heart . . . the doctrine in which our religion is contained must enter our heart and pass into our daily living and so transform us . . . (3:6-4)

We are consecrated and dedicated to God in order that we may thereafter think, speak, meditate and do nothing except to his glory. (3:7-1)

We seek not the things that are ours but these which are of the Lord's will and will serve to advance his glory . . . almost forgetful of ourselves, surely subordinating our self-concern, we try faithfully to devote our zeal to God . . . it not only erases from our minds the yearning to possess, the desire for power and the favor of men, but it also uproots ambition and all craving for human glory and other more secret plagues. (3:7-2)

Unless you give up all thought of self ('this most deadly pestilence of love of self, [3:7-4]) and, so to speak, get out of yourself, you will accomplish nothing here. (3:7-5)

In seeking either the convenience or the tranquility of the present life, Scripture calls us to resign ourselves and all our possessions to the Lord's will. (3:7-8)

For Calvin, who compares favorably with the deepest, grounded spirituality in these above excerpts, "our lives [are] under a continual cross." (3:8-2) The cross is a medicine to remedy our pride, sent by the heavenly physician. (3:8-6) The role of the cross for daily Christian living is stated in these words: "For overturning that good opinion which we falsely entertain concerning our own strength, and unmasking our hypocrisy, which affords us delight, the cross strikes at our perilous confidence in the flesh. It teaches us, thus humbled, to rest upon God alone, with the result that we do not faint or yield. Hope, moreover, follows victory in so far as the Lord, by performing what he has promised, establishes his truth for the time to come. Even if these were the only reasons, it plainly appears how much we need the practice of bearing the cross. (3:8-3)

Just as Calvin filled a number of roles in the practical Christianity of his time, he also authored a number of different types of writings. It must be recognized that his marvelous *Institutes* is not his only literary production. Calvin also wrote in other genres. His commentaries on nearly every book of the Bible provide us with detailed vignettes of his exegetical acumen and his practical orientation. Calvin believed in the consistent preaching-teaching of Scripture. As he would study through a book of the Bible, he would also write out his expositions. That he was concerned to record his exegesis of Scripture, not only leaves the student with a repository of Calvin's own thought on specific passages, but further illumines his commitment to explain Biblical Christianity in practical language. Calvin's commentaries illustrate the heart and devotion of the pastor and the skill of the exegete. Had he not desired to broadcast the truths of Scripture he would not have penned what is today contained in one of the most exhaustive sets of commentaries on both Testaments. Calvin's commentaries are as practical and complete as those written by Hendriksen, McClaren, Ryle and less extensive than those by Spurgeon, Lenski *et al.* Yet it is Calvin who is stigmatized as impractical, rationalistic and un-devotional, while some of these others are championed as inspirational.

Below is a short summary and biblical support of the so-called:

Five Points of Calvinism

The five points of Calvinism take their starting point in Holland in the year 1610. James Arminius, a Dutch professor, had just died and his teaching had been formulated into five main points of doctrine by his followers—known as Arminians [note: not Armenians, citizens of Armenia]. Up to this point, the churches of Holland, in common with the other major Protestant churches of Europe, had subscribed to the Belgic and Heidelberg Confessions of Faith, which were both set squarely on Reformation teachings. The Arminians wanted to change this position, however, and they presented their five points in the form of a Remonstrance—or protest—to the Dutch Parliament. The Five Points of Arminianism were, broadly speaking, as follows:

1. *Free will or human ability.* This taught that man, although affected by the Fall, was not totally incapable of choosing spiritual good, and was able to exercise faith in God in order to

receive the gospel and thus bring himself into possession of salvation.

2. *Conditional election.* This taught that God laid his hands upon those individuals who, he knew—or foresaw—would respond to the gospel. God elected those that he saw would want to be saved of their own free will and in their natural fallen state— which was, of course, according to the first point of Arminianism, not completely fallen anyway.

3. *Universal redemption, or general atonement.* This taught that Christ died to save all men, but only in a *potential* fashion. Christ's death enabled God to pardon sinners, but only on condition that they believed.

4. *The work of the Holy Spirit in regeneration limited by the human will.* This taught that the Holy Spirit, as he began to work to bring a person to Christ, could be effectually resisted and his purposes frustrated. He could not impart life unless the sinner was willing to have this life imparted.

5. *Falling from grace.* This taught that a saved man could fall finally from salvation. It is, of course, the logical and natural outcome of the system. If man must take the initiative in his salvation, he must retain responsibility for the final outcome.

The Five Points of Arminianism were presented to the Sate and a National Synod of the church was called to meet in Dort in 1618 to examine the teaching of Arminius in the light of the Scriptures. The Synod of Dort sat for 154 sessions over a period of seven months, but at the end could find no ground on which to reconcile the Arminian viewpoint with that expounded in the Word of God. Reaffirming the position so unmistakably put forth at the Reformation, and formulated by the French theologian John Calvin, the Synod of Dort formulated its Five Points of Calvinism to counter the Arminian system. These are sometimes set forth in the form of an acrostic on the word, "TULIP," as follows:

T   Total Depravity (i.e., Total Inability)
U   Unconditional Election
L   Limited Atonement (i.e., Particular Redemption)
I   Irresistible Grace (Calling)

P   Perseverance of the Saints.

As can be readily seen, these set themselves in complete opposition to the Five Points of Arminianism. Man is totally unable to save himself on account of the Fall in the Garden of Eden being a *total* fall. If unable to save himself, then God must save. If God must save, then God must be free to save whom he will. If God has decreed to save whom he will, then it is for those that Christ made atonement on the Cross. If Christ died for them, then the Holy Spirit will effectually call them into that salvation. If salvation then from the beginning has been of God, the end will also be of God and the saints will persevere to eternal joy.

We shall see the truth that Charles Haddon Spurgeon meant when he declared, "It is no novelty, then, that I am preaching; no new doctrine. I love to proclaim those strong old doctrines that are nicknamed *Calvinism*, but which are surely and verily the revealed truth of God as it is in Christ Jesus."

Total Depravity

Surely the thing that should impress us is the fact that this system begins with something that must be fundamental in the matter of salvation, and that is, a correct assessment of the *condition* of the one who is to be saved. If we have deficient and light views about sin, then we are liable to have defective views regarding the means necessary for the salvation of the sinner. If we believe that the fall of man in the Garden of Eden was merely partial, then we shall most likely be satisfied with a salvation that is attributable partly to man and partly to God. The words of J. C. Ryle are helpful: "There are very few errors and false doctrines of which the beginning may not be traced up to unsound views about the corruption of human nature. Wrong views of a disease will always bring with them wrong views of a remedy. Wrong views of the corruption of human nature will always carry with them wrong views of the grand antidote and cure of that corruption."

Fully aware that this was the case, the theologians of the Reformation and those who formulated the Reformed teaching into these Five Points at the Synod of Dort, basing their findings firmly on the Scriptures, pronounced that man's natural state is a state of total depravity and therefore, there was a total inability on the part of man to gain, or contribute to, his own salvation.

The whole personality of man has been affected by the Fall, and sin extends to the whole of the faculties—the will, the understanding, the affections and all else. We believe this to be irrefutably taught by the Word of God, as demonstrated in the Scriptures below. According to the biblical testimony, man, by nature, is:

- Dead (Rom. 5:12)
- Bound (2 Tim. 2:25 ff)
- Blind and deaf (Mark 4:11f)
- Uninstructable (1 Cor. 2:14)
- Naturally sinful: (a) by birth (Ps. 51:5) and (b) by practice (Gen. 6:5).

We must ask, then: Can the dead (Eph. 2:1) raise themselves? Can the bound (see Lazarus) free themselves? Can the blind give themselves sight, or the deaf hearing? Can slaves redeem themselves? Can the uninstructable teach themselves? Can the naturally sinful change themselves? Surely not! "Who can bring a clean thing out of an unclean?" (Job 14:4).

Unconditional Election

Our acceptance or rejection of total depravity as a true biblical statement of man's condition by nature will largely determine our attitude towards the next point that came under review at the Synod of Dort. The same truth was set forth in other creeds, namely in the 1689 Baptist Confession of Faith, which affirms: "Those of mankind who are predestinated unto life, God, before the foundation of the world was laid, according to his eternal and immutable purpose, and the secret counsel and good pleasure of his will, hath chosen in Christ unto everlasting glory, out of his mere free grace and love, without any other thing in the creature as a condition or cause moving him thereunto."

The doctrine of unconditional election follows naturally from the doctrine of total depravity. If man is, indeed, dead, held captive, and blind etc., then the remedy for all these conditions must lie outside man himself [that is, with God]. If some people are raised out of their spiritual death, and since they are unable to perform this work for themselves, then we must conclude that it was God who raised them. If man is unable to save himself on account of the Fall in Adam being a *total* fall, and if God alone can save, and if *all* are not saved, then the conclusion must be that God has not chosen to save all.

The story of the Bible is the story of unconditional election. One can easily consult the narratives about Abraham being called out of heathenism, or Israel selected as a peculiar people (Dt. 7:7), or Jacob chosen in place of the elder Esau (Rom. 9-11). Moreover, our Lord himself spoke about this topic three times in Matthew 24 and also in John 15:6. Of course, this doctrine is also alluded to in passages such as Romans 9:15-21 and Ephesians 1:4-5.

For those who try to transform God's election into a mere foreknowing of man's choice to accept the Savior—a good work on man's part by any calculation—the following points should be considered.

1. God's foreknowledge is spoken of in connection with a people and not in connection with any action which people performed. That is to say, irrespective of any action, good or bad, performed by them, God "knew" them in the sense that he loved them and chose them to be his own. It is thus that he foreknew his elect.
2. We are not chosen because we perform such a holy work as "accepting" Christ, but we are chosen so that we might be able to "accept" him (See Eph. 2:10).
3. Neither will it do to say that God foresaw those who would believe (See Acts 13:48). Election is not on account of our believing, but our believing is on account of our being elected.

4. The faith to believe in Christ is given to us by God's regenerating grace. It is the gift of God (Eph. 2:8-9), and it is not of ourselves.

Limited Atonement

This third point not only brings us to the central point of the five, but also to the central fact of the gospel, that is the purpose of Christ's death on the Cross. This is not accidental. The theologians who had set themselves the task of defending the truths of the Protestant Reformation against the attacks of the Arminian party were following a biblical and logical line in their formulations. Since the Bible taught that man, in his natural state, is totally unable to save himself, but that some are undoubtedly saved, the question is "how can any who are saved be saved?" The answer is that the atonement by Christ is stronger than man's sin nature, and it is applied particularly to those God has chosen. This atonement was accomplished through Christ's voluntary submission to the death on the Cross where he suffered under the justice of the Just God and procured the salvation that he as Savior had ordained. On the Cross, then, Christ bore punishment and procured salvation.

The question logically arises: *whose* punishment did Christ bear, and *whose* salvation did he procure? There are three avenues along which we can travel with regard to this:

1. Christ died to *save all men* without distinction. The ***Univeralist*** view believes that all men will be saved.
2. Christ died to *save no one in particular*. The ***Arminian*** view believes that Christ merely procured a potential salvation for those who will eventually choose that anyway. Christ died on the Cross but although he paid the debt of our sin, his work on the Cross does not become effectual until one "decides for" Christ and is thereby saved.
3. Christ died to *save a certain number*. The ***Calvinistic*** view believes that Christ positively died and effectually saved a certain number of hell-deserving sinners on whom the Father had already set his free electing love. The Son paid

the debt for these elect ones, satisfies the Father's justice for them, and imputes his own righteousness to them so that they are complete in him.

Christ's death, then could only have been for one of these three reasons: to save *all*; to save *no one in particular*, to save *a particular set*. Particular redemption understands that Christ died to save a particular number of sinners, i.e., those chosen in him before the foundation of the world (Eph. 1:4); those whom the Father had given him out of the world (Jn. 17:9); those for whom he shed his blood to gain remission of their sins (Mt. 26:28 and Mt. 1:21).

This Calvinistic view alone does justice to the purpose of Christ's coming to this earth to die on the Cross. See Eph. 5:25; Rom. 4:25; 1 Cor. 15:22; Is. 53:11.

We do not overlook the fact that there are some Scriptures, which refer to the "world," and many have taken these as their starting point in the question of Redemption. However, when we compare Scripture with Scripture (as suggested by WCF 1:9), we see that the use of the word "world" need not always imply "every man and woman in the whole world." (See, e.g., Jn. 6:37)

Irresistible Grace

This fourth point of the Calvinistic system of belief is the logical outcome of all that has preceded. If men are unable to save themselves on account of their fallen nature, and if God has purposed to save them, and Christ has accomplished their salvation, then it logically follows that God must also provide the means for calling them into the benefits of that salvation which he has procured for them. The Calvinistic system of theology, however, although soundly logical, is more than a system of mere logic. It is a system of pure biblical belief and must rise or fall with a comparison of its tenets and Scripture.

In a *Tabletalk* article ("Dead Men Walking," June 2002, pp. 6-7), R. C. Sproul provides a clear discussion of irresistible grace. It depends, he argues, on two main foundations: (1) grace as unmerited favor—if we ever earned it, it would be justice; and (2)

God's regeneration as the operation of grace in our lives by the Holy Spirit. Jesus frequently spoke of the necessity of regeneration, but later Semi-Pelagians sought to emphasize a greater human contribution to salvation. These Pelagian cousins presented salvation as synergistic (literally "to work together") in contrast to our Augustinian-Reformed pedigree, which presents grace as the work of God alone. It is only God that can give grace by his divine regeneration, and until that happens, the human being is completely passive, as the WCF affirms elsewhere. Sproul notes that we are as passive as Lazarus was before his resurrection or as Adam was before his creation. Sproul further clarifies:

> Regeneration is not a joint venture. We do not cooperate in it because we will not cooperate in spiritual matters while we are still dead in our sins. Our hearts are totally disinclined and indisposed to the things of God. We love darkness and will not have God in our thinking. . . . We will never choose Christ until or unless we are liberated from that slavery. In short, we are morally unable to exercise faith until and unless we are first regenerated. This is why the axiom of Reformed theology is that regeneration precedes faith. Rebirth is a necessary pre-condition for faith. Faith is not possible for spiritually dead creatures. Therefore, we contend that apart from spiritual rebirth there can be no faith.

> At the same time, the doctrine of irresistible grace teaches that all who are regenerated indeed come to faith. The 'irresistible' may be better described as 'effectual.' All of God's grace is resistible in the sense that sinners resist it. But the saving grace of regeneration is called irresistible because our resistance to it cannot and does not overpower it. The grace of regeneration is effectual in that the effect God the Holy Spirit intends to produce actually does come to pass. When the Holy Spirit supernaturally and immediately works to create a person anew, that person is created anew one hundred times out of one hundred. All who receive this grace are changed. All are liberated from the bondage to sin. All are brought to saving faith. The outcome of this work never depends upon the work of the unregenerate flesh. The grace is operative, not co-operative.

Once that divinely-effected rebirth is worked by God alone (monergism), the "rest of the Christian life is synergistic. But the transformation of the person from death to life, darkness to light, bondage to liberty is done by God alone, effectually and irresistibly," which is why we confess *soli Deo Gloria.*

In the same issue of *Tabletalk*, Al Mohler notes the practical value of this biblical teaching: "The denial of irresistible grace leads to a human-centered understanding of the Gospel, produces pride in the hearts of sinners, and encourages manipulation in evangelism. We are heralds assigned to preach a message, not salesmen charged to market a product." (p. 16)

Perseverance of the Saints

The doctrine of the perseverance of the saints is as precious to the believer as it is biblically clear. Some man-made theologies that award more determination to the will of man than to the will of God have difficulty reconciling this biblical teaching with the clear scriptural testimony. However, it is quite clear that when God begins a good work in us, he sees it to completion—all the way until the time of Jesus' return (Phil. 1:6). This and many other passages put this doctrine within the reach of every believer who will avail himself to God's Word on the subject.

Among the verses we have found helpful on this topic are:

- Romans 8:32-39
- Col. 1:13
- John 10: 27-29
- John 6:54
- 1 Pet. 1:4-5

This comforting biblical teaching is based on several things. It understands regeneration as causing a permanent change in our nature (Jn. 3:1-8). Also, since Christ's death was all-sufficient (Heb. 9:25-28), once he atones for our sin, there is no reversal of that. So certain is our standing with Christ once he adopts us that, as Romans 8 tells us, nothing, no scenario or combination of events—not even stupendous things like "death nor life, neither angels nor demons, neither the present nor future, nor any powers, neither height nor depth, nor anything else in all creation, will be able to separate us from the love of God that is in Christ Jesus our Lord" (Rom. 8:38-39). Those in whom God begins his work of salvation, those who are called, justified, and elected, will also stay with God until the end, to glorification (Rom. 8:30).

John Calvin certainly did not discover or invent this doctrine; God himself reveals it. And its comfort and implications are large for believers and Officers in the church. This gift permits sincere and tender consciences from worrying if God, like many fickle human lovers, will one day fail to be our Saving Spouse. But the more we know the salvation which our God brings, the more clearly we see that he will be faithful to the end, that he will not deny himself (2 Tim. 2:13), and that we can be assured that "If we died with him, we will also live with him; if we endure, we will also reign with him" (2 Tim. 2:11-12).

Of interest to historians, both sympathetic and unsympathetic to Calvin, whatever Calvin was doing transformed Geneva into a visible and bustling forum for economic development. With a growing intellectual ferment, evidenced by the founding of Calvin's Academy, and the presence of modern financial institutions, Geneva became an ideal center for perfecting and exporting reform.[33]

---

[33] Several studies detail Calvin's Geneva. Among the best are: E. William Monter, *Calvin's Geneva* (New York: John Wiley & Sons, 1967); Alastair Duke *et al*, eds., *Calvinism in Europe, 1540-1610: A Collection of Documents* (Manchester, UK: Manchester University Press, 1988); J. T. McNeill, "John Calvin on Civil Government," *Calvinism and the Political Order*, George L. Hunt, ed. (Philadelphia: Westminster Press, 1965), 22-45; William A. Dunning, *A History of Political Theories: From Luther to Montesquieu* (Macmillan, 1919), 26-33; W. Fred Graham, *The Constructive Revolutionary: John Calvin, His Socio-Economic Impact* (Richmond, VA: John Knox Press, 1975); William G. Naphy, *Calvin and the Consolidation of the Genevan Reformation* (Manchester, UK: Manchester University Press, 1994). Two recent biographies also add to our understanding: William Bouwsma's *John Calvin: A Sixteenth-Century Portrait* (New York: Oxford University Press, 1988) and Alister McGrath, *A Life of John Calvin* (Oxford: Basil Blackwell, 1990).

Despite the rise of commerce, however, the story of Calvin's leadership and impact on the region was not primarily economic. The translation of the Reformed faith into practice is witnessed by the creation of tell-tale social structures that emerged from the leadership of Farel and Calvin. A hospital was launched in 1535, and a fund for French refugees (*Bourse Francaise*) was established by church deacons in 1541. Calvin's Academy was founded in 1558. Eventually, thousands of refugees (mainly French, English, and Italian) came to Geneva for shelter; and many later returned to their own lands with fresh ideas about the relationship of citizens to government.[34]

A rediscovery of Calvin's thought, which formed such enduring institutions, might help many students today.

---

[34] See also Jeannine E. Olson's "Social Welfare and the Transformation of Polity in Geneva," John B. Roney and Martin I. Klauber, *The Identity of Geneva: The Christian Commonwealth, 1564-1864* (Westport, CT: Greenwood Press, 1998), 155-168.

Chapter 6

John Bunyan's *Pilgrim's Progress*

Hebrews 11:13-16; Philippians 3:12-16

What comes to mind when you think of Thanksgiving, that uniquely American holiday? Pilgrims, of course. I'm not aware of any other countries that celebrate this holiday, an enduring testimony to the religious impulse in early America. In fact, we have moved so far away from our early heritage that it boggles the mind to imagine today the President and Congress calling on the citizenry to set aside a full day for worship, prayers and thanksgiving. Why, if that were done, certain advocacy groups would hit the roof. We've come that far in three and a half centuries and many call that "progress." America was settled by people who we call pilgrims. Of course, the early settlers of America are not the only ones who've ever been pilgrims. Many people, of many different faiths have been pilgrims. Muslims still take pilgrimages today.

Perhaps the best selling Christian book behind Bible is *Pilgrim's Progress*. If you've never read it, it is well worth your time. Buy a copy at any Christian bookstore and keep a copy in your home. I once had a lady in a church, whose hometown was Bedford, England; there is a monument in a town square that the children refer to as "Ol Bunnywhigs," because it depicts Bunyan in a whig, the style of the day.

However, most of us would do well to know a little something about the life of John Bunyan. Not only was he one of the best selling authors in Christian history, but moreover, he still has much to say to us today.

John Bunyan (1628-1688) was a British Puritan writer and preacher who lived at the time when the American pilgrims landed on our shores. Born at Elstow, near Bedford, into a poor home, he probably acquired his grasp of the English language from reading the Bible. While still a teenager, he supported Cromwell in the Civil War, serving in the Roundhead army.[35]

In 1649 he married, and his wife brought him Dent's *Plain Man's Pathway to Heaven* and Beyly's *Practice of Piety*. In 1653 he joined an Independent church [one that was not a part of the state-established Church of England] at Bedford. A year or two later he began to preach with some success until the local governor arrested him for preaching without proper credentials. He was intermittently in prison from 1660 to 1672, but he used the time to compose *Pilgrim's Progress* and other writings. While he was imprisoned for preaching, he evaluated, re-evaluated, was tested and re-tested to find what was important and to weed that out the primary from the secondary. He tried to emphasize only that which was truly Christian. Prison may have had an effect similar to that once described by Samuel Johnson who said, "When a man knows he is to be hanged in a fortnight it concentrates his mind wonderfully." During these years, Bunyan—like Joseph in an earlier time—had his Christian faith strengthened and refined. Upon release in 1672 he spent most of his time in preaching and evangelism in the Bedford area.

Bunyan was an itinerant handyman, frequently working to repair shoes. His three primary works were: *Pilgrim's Progress* (1678, 1684), *The Holy War* (1682), and *Grace Abounding to the Chief of Sinners* (1666). *Pilgrim's Progress* (along with Foxe's *Book of Martyrs*) was read in virtually every Victorian home, and remains a best seller for children and adults alike.

---

[35] Source for this biography is the *NIDCC*, 167.

Bunyan was a Puritan who held the Calvinist view of grace, but he was a separatist in his views of baptism and the church.

D. Martyn Lloyd-Jones commented: "Bunyan thought of himself essentially as a preacher and as a pastor. He wrote books because he was a pastor and because he wanted to help the poor people who were members of his church in Bedford."[36] He was not an academic; he had very little formal education (391). John Bunyan was a big-natured man, a generous man, a loving man, a man whose interest was not merely academic. (391) He had a profound concern of soul for the ordinary man.

Pilgrim's Progress is an allegory about the journey of saints and living out the gospel. That is, it is a story that is not literal in every detail. It is a story designed to make a point by comparing characters to real-life situations. In *Pilgrim's Progress*, the main character is Pilgrim. Some of you may have read this and felt as though Bunyan's pilgrim was very similar to your own spiritual journey.

Bunyan could have, if he'd chosen, named this:

- Theologian's Progress
- Activist's Progress
- Quiet Timer Progress
- Evangelist's Progress
- Or any others.

But he didn't. He chose 'pilgrim' as his chief metaphor. In his mind, this was the summation of the Christian life—a disciple wandering on his/her way to another homeland. As well as anything else, the idea of a pilgrim captures what Bunyan (and countless others) thought of the Christian life. As Christians, we must constantly recall that we are on a pilgrimage and not settled.

At the outset Pilgrim walks through a wilderness and falls into a dream. He sees himself "clothed with rags" (Is. 64:6 contains the basis of this metaphor: "All our righteousness is as filthy rags.") This pilgrim had on his back a great burden, a burden of sin. As he reads the book (Bible), he weeps, trembles, and cries out, "What

---

[36] D. Martyn Lloyd-Jones, *The Puritans* (Banner of Truth, 1987), 390.

shall I do?" He is miserable under the weight of sin and tells his wife that he and his whole city "will be burned from fire from heaven," if some escape is not found. His family thought that he had some fever and hoped that going to bed would help. But after a night's sleep, the next morning Pilgrim's condition was worse. They called a doctor. His condition did not improve; only his conviction. And while reading the book and asking, 'What shall I do to be saved?" a man named Evangelist came to him. Pilgrim explained, "Sire I perceive by the book in my hand that I am condemned to die, and after that to come to judgment; and I find that I am not willing to do the first nor able to do the second." Then said Evangelist, "Why not willing to die, since this life is attended with so many evils?" Pilgrim answered, "Because I fear that this burden that is upon my back will sink me lower than the grave." Evangelist then pointed the way to a journey that would provide the answer. Are you beginning to see what an apt analogy this is of salvation and Christian living?

Pilgrim was to follow the light. Along the way, various neighbors, e. g., Obstinate and Pliable, tried to dissuade Pilgrim from his journey. Pilgrim was fleeing the City of Destruction, and his name has been changed to "Christian," signifying that true conversion has occurred. His goal is the Heavenly city, the New Jerusalem, Mount Zion.

Along the way, Christian faced many difficulties, such as the slough of Despond where Pliable deserted him in the face of affliction. Here's what Pilgrim found "As the sinner is awakened about his lost condition, there arises in his soul many fears and doubts, and discouraging apprehensions. . ." (p. 8)[37] Isn't that true: After you're led to Christ, it is only then that you begin to see some fears?

Next along the way, Christian meets Worldly Wiseman from the town of Carnal Policy. Worldly Wiseman sought to distract Christian by (a) pointing him to morality and (b) shrinking the death of Christ on the cross. Worldly Wiseman "is an alien" (16), Mr.

---

[37] Page numbers in parentheses refer to the Christian Library edition (Barbour, 1989.

Legality is a cheat; and for his son, Civility . . . he is a hypocrite."
(16). These are typical of those who wear the mask of religion
today, only to offer non-solutions.

Finally, Christian goes up the way of Salvation, but with great
difficulty because of the load on his back. Here's how he got that
load off his back: "He ran thus till he came at a place somewhat
ascending; and upon that place stood a cross, and a little below, in
the bottom, a sepulchre. . . . just as Christian came up with the cross,
his burden loosed from off his shoulders, and fell from off his back
and began to tumble, and so continued to tumble till it came to the
mouth of the sepulchre, where it fell in, and I saw it no more."
"Then was Christian glad and merry. . . . Then he stood still awhile
to look and wonder; for the ease of his burden. He looked, therefore,
and look again, even till the springs that were in his head sent the
waters down his cheeks." Three "Shining Ones" came to him; the
first said, "Thy sins be forgiven thee, the second stripped him of his
rags , . . the third also set a mark on his forehead." (30) and sings a
song of joy. He is saved and he knows it.

Then begins the pilgrimage. Remember this: Conversion/New
Life precede the pilgrimage; not vice-versa. We do not set out on a
religious trek until God first comes into our life. We cannot work
our way to preparation for salvation.

Can any of you relate to this? I can.

Isn't this a fitting portrait of salvation? We have struggled and
struggled throughout life, with a huge pack of sins on our backs. We
are weighed down and cannot possibly move until that pack is
removed. Jesus takes it off our backs and discards it, casts it into the
mouth of the Sepulcher where he was buried. Then and only then
have our sins rolled away. He takes the burden for us and disposes
of it.

Then our new life in Christ begins; we are pilgrims hence.

Some of the characters we—and pilgrim—meet along the way
are: Simple, Presumption, Sloth, Form, Ignorance and Hypocrisy.
He flees Vain-Glory and Vanity Fair. He is tempted by the Giant of
Despair and the Delectable Mountains, but sets his course on.

Others such as Temporary, Ignorance, Talkative, Flatterer, Little-Faith encounter him as he goes through the Valley of the Shadow of death, Vanity Fair ("no new-erected business, but a thing of ancient standing" (80), and Broad-way or Deadman's Lane. These are typical temptations of Christian living today.

One of the outstanding things about *Pilgrim's Progress* is its view of sin. This book teaches us that sin is what weighs us down and must be put to death. Without crucifying sin, we will not live the holy life that God desires. Holiness of life is not to be confused with how many theological opinions a person knows. "A holy life, not opinions, is the beauty of Christianity. . . It is, then, because every man makes too much of his own opinion, abounds too much in his own sense, and takes not care to separate his opinion from the error he clings to."[38]

Why is this still helpful for us today? Precisely because the two words in the title are so important for each Christian today. Let me focus on them with you, and have you review some Scriptures with me. First think of the word, pilgrim.

Pilgrim

The OT Feasts remind the people that they are Pilgrims in the Land. During the Babylonian Exile and while wandering in the wilderness, God wanted his people—on more than one occasion—to recall that they were pilgrims, in transition.

One Feast in particular made this point vividly: the Feast of Booths/ Tabernacles. In this feast, once a year, the people of Israel would leave the comforts of home and camp-out for a week. They erected crude lean-to like booths, only made to last temporarily. These temporary booths reminded them to be thankful for their own homes. They had not always had such comfort, and God thought it wise to remind people annually not to take their comforts for granted. Living out in those booths taught the people to remember their dependence on God and to be thankful for the many creature comforts they/we have. This was an exercise in

---

[38] Lloyd-Jones, *The Puritans*, 396.

creating a thankful spirit by frequently doing without. It is sometimes only when we do without that we become most thankful.

Have you done that lately? Why not dwell on the many comforts God has given you. Don't take those for granted. Remember this next thanksgiving.

This feast also reminded the people that they were not of this world; they had a final home, alright, but it wasn't in this world. In fact, if we become too comfortable in this world, that is a sign of lax affection for Christ.

Hebrews 11:13-16 makes it clear that even the OT saints understood this: "All these people were still living by faith when the died . . . they only received them at a distance. And they admitted that they were aliens and strangers on earth."

A list of heroes of the faith is provided in Hebrews 11. Amidst a discussion of how Abraham had faith, the Book of Hebrews notes that the OT saints were living by faith when they died. They had true faith, just like we do today. When they died they had not received all the things God had promised to bring about. Some of those were still future. These OT saints had learned to be content and wait on the fulfillment of all God's promises.

Hebrews 11:13 even tells that they admitted that they were "aliens and strangers" on earth. They were pilgrims.

John Owen said: "[T]hey avowedly professed that their interest was not in nor of this world . . . they publicly renounced [love for] the world like other men whose portion is in this life. This renunciation of all things beside Christ in the promise is an eminent act of faith . . . The world is the home, the country, the city . . . of most men; but it is not so with believers; they are strangers and pilgrims, sojourners in the world for a season . . . they sought another country . . . 'a better country' which could be none other but a heavenly." (Commentary on Hebrews, 225) They had opportunity to return, but the allure and enjoyments of this world did not tempt them. "They had an earnest, active desire that put them on all due ways and means of attaining it. This desire includes a sense of [dissatisfaction] unsatisfiedness in things present; a just apprehension of the worth of the things desires; also a sight of the way whereby it may be attained. . . . Heaven is the desire in the bottom of the sighs and groans of all believers, whatever outwardly may give occasion to them."

The scripture teaches us that the saints before us were "looking for a country of their own." They had not come into possession of that final home. The author of Hebrews suggests: "If they had been thinking of the country they had left, they would have had opportunity to return. Instead, they were longing for a better country—a heavenly one." (Heb. 11:15-16a). These previous saints were pilgrims. They realized that whatever earthly comforts were afforded, God had a better home for us. They knew not to put too much stock in the present values, fads, or accomplishments of this city. Their true citizenship was elsewhere; above in the heavenly Jerusalem. They refused to allow themselves to become at home, accustomed, to this world. These earlier pilgrims stubbornly refused to settle down here in this or any other worldly city. Why? Because they knew the superiority of God's city; they knew that the riches of God were far more valuable and lasting than anything this world could afford. They were not entranced, addicted to the comforts of this life. These spiritual expatriates had "a single-minded commitment [with] no thought of turning back." (P. E. Hughes, *in loc.*)

As a result, God himself identified with them: "Therefore, God is not ashamed to be called their God, for he has prepared a city for them." All of the OT saints and NT saints combined, form a nation—a nation of pilgrims who are on the way to permanent citizenship. We are "in the world, but not of this world."

Philippians 3:20 says, "But our citizenship is in heaven, and we eagerly await a Savior from there . . ."

The contrast that God wanted to draw was between a pilgrim and a settled person. Think about it just a moment. A settled person is one, like most of us, who lives in the same home, normally does the same thing, and has a routine. Routines are not all bad. In fact, in some ways they are quite helpful.

However, it is a temptation that in the routines of life, one may lose some of the dependence on God. It is possible to become lulled into thinking that we ourselves are providing, or that we have created our own little kingdom. Are you too comfort-able, too settled? Knowing that full well, God designed some regular reminders. In the OT, once a year, he had the people revisit an earlier time in their history when they did not have it so well—when they walked more in moment by moment dependence. God planned for the people to be pilgrims again. In that temporary feast, they remembered what it was like to be poor, to do without, and other things that are good for us. Maybe we need such routines. Every Lord's Day should have some aspect of remembering our dependence on God and the temporary nature of this world.

A pilgrim was one on a journey. This pilgrim left his home and went to places that were difficult—think of how little comfort, security, or safety our American pilgrim forefathers had. All along the way, the pilgrim has little to refresh; the journey is rough. Yet, the pilgrim treks on. Why? Because the homeland, or the future homeland is superior even to the privation in this life.

That's true for the Christian. For us, when something bad befalls us, we do not give up—for we know that this is not our final home. When others around us are addicted to material comfort, we know the surpassing excellence of God and things of eternity. When we have a victory, we also need to remember that it will be a fading one. We're on the way to heaven, but not there in this world.

'Progress' is the other word to keep in mind.

Sanctification has a definitive, non-repeatable aspect. In one sense, we are made as holy as we possibly can be at conversion. However, there is another sense in which we are clearly called on to grow in holiness. God wants us growing in our Christian faith. There is an undeniable part of Christianity that deals with moving ahead, pressing toward the goal. We will do that all our life. As Paul indicated, he had not already reached perfection, but pressed on toward that.

Philippians 3:12-16 talks about this when the Apostle Paul affirms that he has not already been totally perfected, nor had he obtained all spiritual growth: "Brother," he said, "I do not consider myself yet to have taken hold of it. . . I press on toward the goal to win the prize for which God has called me heavenward."

All of cosmic history is moving toward that goal. It will not be realized until the time of our Lord's return, but nonetheless, history is going somewhere. Not only our lives, but the life of the world is marching to God's drumbeat. There is advance and progress. Even though at times even the most mature of saints question whether or not we're recycling the same errors of the past, still we are moving as God wants us to. We are to press ahead. Growth and progress is part of God's will for us. Sure, it may not be uniform, nor occur at a constant rate, but God leads us ahead and calls us to progress. There is such a thing as Christian growth and increase in holiness—at least growth in the sense that we do not stumble at all the same points that we used to.

In *Pilgrim's Progress*, Christian begins his race while he is very weak. His understanding is low, his courage is sparse, and his commitment is new. As he walks longer toward the celestial city, however, he grows in discernment, he begins to doubt Talkative, By-ends (a get along kind of guy), and does not fall for all the temptations he would at an earlier stage.

One of the famous sections of *Pilgrim's Progress* is the description of Vanity Fair. Christian must pass through Vanity Fair and resist its temptations prior to entering the Celestial City. When pilgrim sets foot in Vanity Fair, he stands out. Pilgrim is known by his clothing—he is dressed in the robes of righteousness. He also spoke the "native language of Canaan"—his speech is different from other worldly-minded people. Also, his interests are different. Pilgrim is not interested (as are other people of the world) in honor, riches, land, pleasures, ease, or lust. And guess what? The residents of Vanity Fair mock Christian, indict him, question his truthfulness, put him in jail (like Bunyan), humiliate him, and eventually kill his friend, Faithful.

In one section, Prudence asks Christian how he overcomes his difficulties. The Christian Pilgrim answers: "[W]hen I think what I saw at the cross, that will do it; and when I look upon my broidered coat [symbol of robes of righteousness], that will do it; and when I look into the roll [book of life] that I carry . . . that will do it; and when my thoughts wax warm about whither I am going, that will do it." Pilgrim, thus meditates on what God has done for him to be motivated to overcome his difficulties. Prudence then follows-up: "And what is it that makes you so desirous to go to Mount Zion?" Christian answered, "Why, there I hope to see Him alive that did hang dead on the cross; and their I hope to be rid of all those things that to this day are in me and annoyance to me. There they say there is no death, and there I shall dwell with such company as I like best. For, to tell you truth, I love him because I was by Him eased of my burden; and I am weary of my inward sickness. I would fain be where I shall die no more, and with the company that shall continually cry, 'Holy, Holy, Holy.'" (42) That is how we grow in Christ, by often contemplating what Christ has done for us.

Along the way, Christian meets Apollyon [the devil], "the monster was hideous to behold; he was clothed with scales like a fish, and they are his pride; he had wings like a dragon, feet like a bear, and out of his belly came fire and smoke; and his mouth was as the mouth of a lion." (48) By the way, Christian did not meet the devil because he felt strong or was looking for some challenge. Christian actually wanted to flee from the devil. He was in the Valley of Humiliation when he saw Apollyon approach him. Christian was afraid and wanted to go back. He considered that option but remembered that he had no armor for his back, "and therefore thought that to turn the back to him might give him greater advantage with ease to pierce him with his darts; therefore he resolved to venture, and stand his ground." Sometimes, we resist the devil only because we cannot flee.

The devil's temptations are graphically portrayed in this classic. Apollyon informs Christian that he is one of his own subjects, born in his country and that he is Christian's Prince. But the pilgrim answers: "I was born, indeed, in your dominions, but your service was hard, and your wages such as a man could not live on; for the wages of sin is death; therefore when I was come of years, I did, as other considerate persons do . . . if I perhaps might mend myself." But Apollyon will not surrender one of his subjects easily: "There is no prince that will thus lightly lose his subjects, neither will I as yet lose thee; but since you complain of your service and wages, be content to go back, and what[ever] our country will afford, I do here promise to give thee." Such is Satan's temptation to the new convert: he tempts him with better sinful provision. Satan tells him that he will regret it when suffering comes. Still the pursuit of the Celestial City is more valuable than the riches of Satan's country. But there is progress in this Christian's life.

Pilgrim's Progress may also be expressive of the conversion of some.

We nay also come to view life as pilgrimage as opposed to being enamored with this worldliness. Calvin taught that the best way to order our lives in this world is to frequently view God's eternal purposes.

> Let the aim of believers in judging mortal life, then, be that while they understand it to be of itself nothing but misery, they may with greater eagerness and dispatch betake themselves wholly to meditate upon that eternal life to come. When it comes to a comparison with the life to come, the present life can not only be safely neglected but . . . must be utterly despised and loathed. For, if heaven is our homeland, what else is the earth but our place of exile? If departure from the world is entry into life, what else is the world but a sepulcher? And what else is it for us to remain in life but to be immersed in death? If to be freed from the body is to be released into perfect freedom, what else is the body but a prison? (*Institutes*, 716)

Christian's friend, Faithful, sings an exhortation:
The trials that those men do meet withal,
That are obedient to the heavenly call,
Are manifold, and suited to the flesh,
And come, and come, and come again afresh;
That now, or sometimes else, we by them may

Be taken, overcome, and cast away.
    let the pilgrims, let the pilgrims then,
Be vigilant, and quit themselves like men! (66)

Are you on the pilgrim route? All Christians are. One of the essential tenets of Christianity is that we are never at home until we are with the Lord. In 2 Corinthians 5, Paul said it this way: "We groan longing to be clothed with our heavenly dwelling . . . For while we are in this tent, we groan and are burdened . . . as long as we are at home in this body we are away from the Lord . . . we would prefer to be away from the body and at home with the Lord. So we make it our goal to please him, whether we are at home in the body or away from it." That is the goal of the pilgrim: to please God wherever we are on the road. And we are on the road.

If we find ourselves at rest, comfortable, self-assured, then perhaps this notion of pilgrimage will trouble us. God does not call us to fall in love with the things of this world. We are called to be 'on the move.' We are in transit more than we are settled. We are on the way, in process. Can you accept that? What is ahead of us will always be greater than what is behind us.

No matter what age you find yourself . . . No matter where . . . God calls you to be a pilgrim

1 Peter 2:11 teaches this: "Dear friends, I urge you as aliens and strangers in the world to abstain from sinful desires." It as aliens, strangers or pilgrims that we live this life. Get used to the road; and if you ever look up and find that you're not on the way to the Celestial City, then get back on the road.

I've had a curious thought recently: Why no pilgrims today? Did these have stronger faith than we? Perhaps. The pilgrims who discovered America went to great lengths to follow the Lord. Can you see yourself as a pilgrim? An on-the-way Christian?

Chapter 7

Contentment (Jeremy Burroughs): *A Rare Jewel*

Philippians 4:13-17

One of biggest problems in our day is the lack of contentment; it leads to boredom, anxiety, coveting, and bitterness.

Many people are not even aware how damaging the lack of contentment is. I watch people who routinely sleep-walk through life, and appear to be about to die from boredom. Boredom is often the result of over-stimulation. And when that excessive stimulation is over, boredom's claws can grab us around the neck. It is true that many times we cannot keep up with the frenzy of ubiquitous sensationalism. Even evangelical Christians are hounded by this.

Why, some well-meaning Christians don't even know how to deal with the lack of sensuality in worship or life. They complain that they are bored if things are not riveting and full of surround-sound. Some children may be heard to say, as my little niece did once, "That church was pretty, but thems was a little borin'." You know one of the reasons why children say things like that: "Because parents and adults, somehow, lead them to expect that all of life must be stimulating, exciting, and sensibly-popping in order to be good. In the case of the holy things of God, we may create a real problem for ourselves if we allow that idea to persist. Boredom, all along, may be in the eye of the beholder.

Then again in life, listen to some people talk. Many people talk about their jobs as if those are the highest pinnacle of time-wasting. Some people will quit a job because it is boring; others will become embittered on life itself, because the workplace is not as exciting as the Super Bowl. Goodness; what do we expect? Why do you think it's called "work"; it's not called "party." Many complaints of on-the-job boredom might be paraphrased as follows: "I love to party, have fun, be the center of attention, and do things that I enjoy doing. On Mondays through Fridays, from 8:00-5:00 I am not able to do that during that mean old thing called a job (which by the way pays the ticket for all of the rest of one's life), and I don't like non-exciting activity; so I'm bored with life."

Still others may describe life as boring; responsibility as severely curtailing of unbridled self-expression, and duties in general as "unfulfilling." What would happen if all parents ceased to take care of little children, when those parents discovered after the first several hundred diaper changes and night-time feedings, that the routine was pretty much the same every time, and became bored with that? Should they halt providing nurture for their children? If boredom is the supreme value, maybe they should. Or if teachers get tired of the same adolescent pranks and weaknesses, should they stop teaching because of the absence of brilliance or the dearth of stimulating students? Or what if the next time you really need surgery, you show up at the surgeon's office, and are told this: "Dr. Smith will not be in today; he's looked at your X-Rays and he has seen this kind of injury hundreds of times. He's somewhat unfulfilled doing the same thing all the time, and decided to go to the beach and write poetry. He's bored with surgery."

High school students in the summer time are some of the first to become bored. I remember loving the first 7-10 days out of school. Then after you've slept in, consumed more junk food than a few developing nations, and watched all the re-runs, most 15 year olds will say something unbelievably profound like, "I'm bored."

Behind the facade of boredom, in most cases, is an underlying lack of contentment; and it is becoming a massive society-wide epidemic. People can kill themselves by pursuing the always-upward trend of excitement. If a person cannot learn to be content, it will be hard to live. The nagging desire for more, more, more, was called "avarice or greed" by our spiritual grandparents. The enemy of greed is contentment with the lot in life that God gives us. This contentment is almost a rare jewel.

A 17th century puritan, in fact, wrote a book called *The Rare Jewel of Christian Contentment.* I want to focus on this subject and this scriptural teaching in this chapter.

The book, *The Rare Jewel of Christian Contentment*, was written by: Jeremy Burroughs (1599-1646). He was an English non-denominational Christian. He was reformed in his doctrine—so much so that he was a member of the Westminster Assembly. However, due to his bad experience with the Anglican hierarchy, he didn't want to be a part of a connected church structure. He thought each church would be best, if left to its own independence. He practiced what he preached about Christian contentment. He was opposed by ecclesiastical powers, ejected from pulpits, and forced to flee to other countries merely to preach the gospel.

He'd been educated at Emmanuel College, Cambridge—the cradle of British puritanism of that day. His first pastoral work was as an assistant pastor, serving under the well-known and respected, Edmund Calamy at Bury St. Edmunds. He became rector of Tivetshall, Norfolk in 1631. However, his convictions were so strong that he could not remain in the Anglican church. Bishop Wren suspended him in 1636, and he fled to Rotterdam to serve as an assistant (to fellow Westminster Divine, William Bridge) in an English Congregationalist Church. During his five year tenure in Holland, which was a refuge for many puritans during this period, no doubt, Burroughs learned much about contentment. He returned to London in 1641, and served as a lecturer at Stepney and Cripplegate churches.

Jeremiah Burroughs was an "esteemed and great ornament of the pulpit" and was known as the morning star of Stepney, the large congregation he pastored. Burroughs was also a writer of great penetration, handling extensive and difficult subjects with uncommon evangelical piety. Cotton Mather, patriarch of American Christianity, gave great praise for Burroughs, who died at a fairly young age, 47, on Nov 14, 1646. He was known as an excellent scholar, a good expositor, and a popular preacher.

Burroughs has a lasting witness through many of his writings. Not only was he known for his practical commentary on *Hosea* (four volumes!), but also for numerous sermons preached at public thanksgivings and before the House of Peers and the House of Lords in the 1640s. Divisions among Independents and Presbyterians so greatly grieved his heart, that in later life he wrote a plea for unity among Christians, (*Irenicum, to the Lovers of Truth and Peace*) Among his other works were *Gospel Worship: The Right Manner of Sanctifying the Name of God in General* (published posthumously in 1648), and *The Gospel, Two Treatises*, one of which was on "Earthly Mindedness" with the second treatise on the "Exceeding Sinfulness of Sin." Perhaps Burroughs is most widely known for his *The Saints' Treasury* or his sermons on the Beatitudes, *The Saints' Happiness* (both recently reprinted). Burroughs is an enduring example of the union of godly learning with depth of piety.

He had to learn contentment in the church when it was less than pure, while exiled in Holland, while a minority at an important theological colloquy, and the contentment of dying fairly young of cancer before the Confession of Faith was finished.

The apostle Paul spoke about this contentment in Philippians 4:11-12: "I have learned to be content whatever the circumstances. I know what it is to be in need, and I know what it is to have plenty. I have learned the secret of being content in any and every situation, whether well fed or hungry, whether living in plenty or in want."

Paul had times in his life when he was hungry; at others, he was well-fed. He had to learn to accept what God gave him each day; not to depend on what he had the day before or might have the next day.

Paul also knew what it was like to be in need, and to be threatened by lions. Recall his experience recorded in 2 Corinthians 6:4-10: ". . . in great endurance; in troubles, hard-ships and distresses; in beatings, imprisonments and riots; in hard work, sleepless nights and hunger . . . through glory and dishonor, bad report and good report, genuine, yet regarded as imposters; known, yet regarded as unknown; dying, and yet we live on; beaten, and yet not killed; sorrowful, yet always rejoicing; poor, yet making many rich; having nothing, and yet possessing everything." Did you catch that last part: having nothing, and yet possessing everything? Paul did not think of his momentary suffering as the paramount reality. More important to him was the fact of God's grace. Knowing God's grace is the key to contentment. A grace-dominated heart "looks upon every promise as coming from the root of the great Covenant of grace in Christ."[39]

But Paul never complained against God; and he isn't recorded as being bored.

Earlier in the book of Philippians, Paul gave a great illustration of how to convert a huge mess into the Lord's glory. Paul wrote that very Epistle from Roman imprisonment. He had been chained to Roman soldiers, confined from freely moving about, but still he preached the gospel. Listen to what he said in Phil. 1:12-14. What had happened to him, including his imprisonment, ended up advancing the gospel. Because he was in the bowels of the Imperial Capital, although that probably wouldn't have been his first choice for ministry site, he was able to proclaim the gospel to the rulers of the empire, including the "whole praetorian guard." "Because of his chains," the elite troups were being evangelized and other brothers were encouraged to preach more boldly. Paul's contentment with God's providence opened doors for the spread of the gospel.

One of the chief passages on the subject of contentment occurs a few chapters later in Philippians. In Philippians 4:11, Paul affirms that he has learned the "mystery" of contentment. I hope you'll see at least three things from this passage. Contentment is:

(a) **a secret mystery; it is not in the province of nature.**
(b) **learned;**

---

[39] Jeremiah Burroughs, *The Rare Jewel of Christian Contentment* (orig. 1648; Banner of Truth Trust, 1995), 81. All references in parentheses to this edition.

(c) **not dependent on outward circumstances.**

(A) Isn't that interesting to think of contentment as a secret or a 'mystery.' To be well-practiced at this mystery of contentment is, according to Burroughs, "the duty, glory, and excellence of a Christian." It involves a realization that the Christian has a sufficient portion of Christ . . . to satisfy himself in every condition (18). Part of the 'mystery' is this: "A contented man, though he is most contented with the least things in the world, yet he is the most dissatisfied man that lives in the world." (43) One can be content while dissatisfied; content with God, but unaccustomed to the world.

Burroughs wrote: "A Christian comes to contentment, not so much by way of addition, as by way of subtraction." (45) "The mystery consists not in bringing anything from outside to make my condition more comfortable, but in purging out something that is within." (55)

Contentment does not come by possessions—which is the only way the world knows to find contentment—but by surrender. Ambrose (4th century AD) said, "Every poverty itself is riches to holy men." Even affliction does us good. Have you learned the secret of being content, even while under affliction? Like salvation itself, this is by grace alone and not by our works.

To be content is a product of grace in our lives. We do not have this by the state of nature, and one can rarely find lasting contentment present in an unbeliever. Contentment is also hardly noticeable in the state of nature. It is produced in us when we learn of Christ and his superior salvation.

"A gracious heart has learned this art, not only to make the commanding will of God to be its own will—that is, what God commands me to do, I will do it—but to make the providential will of God as the operative will of God to be his will too. . . . A Christian makes over his will to God, and in making over his will to God, he has no other will but God's. Suppose a man were to make over his debt to another man. If the man to whom I owe the debt is satisfied and contented, I am satisfied." (54)

Somewhere amidst all this, contentment gets lost unless one knows the providence of God. To remain content, a person must surrender his will to God's will.

Contentment is "that sweet, inward, quiet, gracious frame of spirit, which freely submits to and delights in God's wise and fatherly disposal in every condition." (19) Do you delight in how God is working his will out in your life? Sometimes, it is difficult for even the best of saints.

In 1 Timothy 6:8, Paul affirmed that having food and clothing, we should be content. Earlier in the same chapter, he'd noted that "godliness with contentment was of great gain." (6:6) Since this is not a part of nature, it belongs to the realm of grace and can only be learned after coming to Christ.

Hebrews 13:5 asserts: "Let your life be without covetousness and be content with such things as you have." Romans 12:12 also includes a clue about contentment. We are to be "joyful in hope, patient in affliction. . ."

One sign of discontent is easy distraction. The Christian ought to be able to stick with tasks and endure difficulty or even inglorious [unglamorous] stations, because we "prize duty more highly than to be distracted by every trivial occasion." (23). "Indeed," said Burroughs, "a Christian values every service of God so much that though some may be in the eyes of the world and of natural reason a slight and empty business, beggarly elements, or foolishness, yet since God calls for it, the authority of the command so overawes his heart that he is willing to spend himself and to be spend in discharging it." (23) Very ordinary works can be glorifying to God. The maturing Christian will learn to value small areas of service to the Great and Mighty God over great and mighty areas of service to the low god of self. Contentment will sooner be found in enjoying God in the small routines of life than in fame and fortune. Christians learn that outward success is not necessarily related to contentment. Even when the tide of success runs low, we have enough in Christ alone to satisfy.

A preacher from an earlier age said, "The Devil loves to fish in troubled waters." (126). By that he meant that, the Devil was most effective when people were troubled, vexed, or upset. The devil may, indeed, have a tougher time working among those who are content, reconciled to "whatever God ordains" as best, and satisfied with what God gives. Focus briefly with me on:

How Jesus Taught Contentment

Luke 3:14 records Jesus' command to soldiers to avoid stealing money and to "Be content with your pay.") In the Gospel of Matthew 6:25-34 our Lord teaches about contentment. He tells us to be satisfied with what God gives us each day. His assumption is that God is enough. Jesus also urged his disciples not to worry about the next day. We are to live in a posture of trust, as the lilies of the field do.

Jesus taught that contentment was related to self-denial. In fact, self-denial was one of the first and most basic of lessons that Jesus taught to his disciples. It was part of the ABCs and one "must learn the lesson of self-denial or you can never become a scholar in Christ's school." (87) Jesus wanted his followers to learn that they were nothing and deserve nothing. In John 15:5, he taught, "Without me you can do nothing." And he meant it. Even the best of Christians, with the best of tools and resources, cannot accomplish anything for Christ, without him. Part of contentment comes in realizing that most of us are not called to be heroes or famous. We have to **learn** to look at ourselves in the mirror and say, "Lord I am nothing; I deserve nothing; I can do nothing apart from you; . . . and if I come to nothing and perish" (89), the world will probably eek by and be just fine. Can you be content in the realization that this world can plod on without you and your efforts? Can you surrender that? If so, contentment may arrive a little sooner.

We need to follow Jesus and be able to say, "This little affliction I am suffering is small when compared to great mercy."

We also need to imitate Jesus in affirming the vanity of the creature. Moreover, the Christian will grow in contentment to the degree that he/she understands that we live in this world as pilgrims, as soldiers in Christ's army, or as servants—not as spoiled royalty. If we suffer, we should not become shocked; if things are difficult, we are not the first for whom things have been difficult; if life does not yield super levels of fun and stimulation, that is not a crisis. We are passing through this world, in some respects. We must not become too attached to this world and its cares or allures.

Contentment is wrapped up with resting in and submitting to God's will. There are few words more hated than "submit." No one wants to use it anymore; nearly every segment of society seems to declare its own *jihad* to eliminate any kind of or reference to 'submit.' Yet, it is a very good and biblical term. "The word 'submit' means [from the Latin] 'to send under.' Thus in one who is discontented the heart will be unruly, and would even get above God so far as discontent prevails. But now comes the grace of contentment and sends it under, for to submit is to send a thing under. Now when the soul comes to see its own unruliness—Is the hand of God bringing an affliction and yet my heart is troubled and discontented—what, it says, will you be above God? Is this not God's hand and must your will be regarded more than God's? O, under, under!! Get under, O Soul. Keep under! Keep Low! Keep under God's feet! You are under God's feet, and keep under his feet! Keep under the authority of God, the majesty of God, the sovereignty of God, the power that God has over you! To keep under, that is to submit." (33)

Contentment cannot be gained without some submission, as it involves "taking pleasure in God's disposal." (33) If we are to be content, we must invariably view God's activity as good. It is right, just, and also GOOD.

Let me briefly mention, by way of contrast The OPPOSITES of Contentment.

A Murmuring Spirit

Jude 14-16 reveals a startling truth about murmuring. While he is describing the ungodliness of sinners, the first instance listed of an ungodly behavior is "murmurers": "to judge everyone, and to convict all the ungodly of all the ungodly acts they have done in the ungodly way, and of all the harsh words ungodly sinners have spoken . . . The men are grumblers and faultfinders; they follow their own evil desires. . ." In God's Word, murmuring is no small sin. It is at the head of this particular catalogue of vice. It was in the OT as well. When we murmur about God, we are rebelling against his providence; we are complaining about how God runs the universe. We ought to learn to recall that God is the king of the universe and that we are the bride of Christ. Jesus is our Elder Brother, we are destined to be above angels, we are one with all the saints, we are the Temple of the Holy Spirit, and we are very members of the Body of Christ. All power in heaven and on earth belongs to him who loves us and gave himself for us. What do we have to murmur about? Murmuring is "below the spirit of a Christian." (148) It is less than what God expects from us or approves.

And from a murmuring spirit flow other ill-effects that do not assist us in serving the Lord. When we murmur, we go contrary to our prayer that God's will be done in our lives. If God's will is produced, and then we don't like it, what does that say about one's prayer? Where does Christ teach us to pray for God's will to be done for a period or in general, but not in particulars? Where does Christ in any way indicate that we are to pray for God's will to be done, if we are satisfied with it?

Burroughs lists the ill-effects of murmuring (153-160):

1. By murmuring and discontent in your hearts, you come to lose a great deal of time; one can waste enormous amounts of time, complaining about what God has done.

2. Murmuring also causes distractions from our duty, and keeps us from doing what God calls us to. If we spend a lot of time grumbling, that subtracts from ways we might serve the Lord.

3. When a person throws a fit of discontent, it leads to other sins and rebellions; it also makes us unhappy.

4. "Unthankfulness is an evil and wicked effect which comes from discontent." (154). Unthankfulness is a great sin. Yet, many a saint is tempted to say that all that God has given is not enough; it is worthless.

I found a fascinating line of thinking from Luther on this subject. Martin Luther said: "The rhetoric of the Spirit of God is to [minimize] extenuate evil things and to amplify good things; if a cross comes, it makes the cross but little, but if there is a mercy, it makes the mercy great." That means that God the Holy Spirit speaks in accents that diminish the significance of suffering or affliction, while extolling the greatness of mercy. "The Spirit of God extenuates evils and crosses, and magnifies and amplifies all mercies; and makes all mercies seem to be great, and all afflictions seem to be little." In contrast, "the Devil . . . lessens God's mercies and amplifies evil things. Thus a godly man wonders at his cross—that it is not more; a wicked man wonders that his cross is so much. . . If there is a cross [suffering], the devil puts the soul to musing on it, and making it greater than it is, and so it brings discontent. And on the other side, if there is a mercy, then it is the rhetoric of the Devil to lessen the mercy. . . . Thus the rhetoric of Satan lessens God's mercies, and increases afflictions." (155-156)

5. Grumbling gives rise to even more distractions in spirit.

In sum, "A discontented spirit, out of envy to God's grace, will make mercies that are great little, [or] to be none at all." (157) Like spoiled children, sometimes even Christians will be heard to protest: Because I cannot have what I want, I will not enjoy what I do have. "Discontent . . . eats out the good and sweetness of a mercy before it comes." (159)

A grumbling spirit is more like the devil than like God. "There is much of the spirit of Satan in a murmuring spirit. The Devil is the most discontented creature in the world, he is the proudest creature that is, and the most discontented creature, and the most dejected creature." (166) To the degree that one is discontent, he has the spirit of Satan. If a person is not content, he will be agitated continually.

Other opposites of contentment are:

Stealing—an outright attempt to seize what God has not given to improve our lot in life. Stealing is the taking of what God has not given. This outward and sinful act is the opposite of contentment; and there are many ways to steal.

However, there is also a hidden, invisible form of stealing that is a distinct opposite of contentment: Covet.

Coveting is the lust to have what God has not given. In every case of coveting, the creature questions the Creator, disagrees with the "rewards" we think we should have, puffs up self in its own eyes, and inwardly wants what another person has. If/when we do not receive what we covet, we become discontent. We may develop a pattern of grumbling, complain excessively, or even act on our inward greed. That's why the Bible equates coveteousness with idolatry: it is the worship of what we do not have.

Coveting and contentment can never cohabitate.

Let me clarify one important thing before concluding: Contentment does not mean becoming a pacifist or resigning from hard work. Nor does it mean that we cannot groan in prayer to God. Neither does contentment imply that a believer can never seek correction or other recourse. It does mean that our soul is more infected with thanks for the providence of God than any physical grumblings.

True Christian contentment is deep and inward; it is unsettled to some extent by particular events. Contentment is part of our character and is not easily shaken.

Godly contentment becomes a part of our habitual character, not merely a flash of mood. God wants his children to be content with what he gives. And when you go through a difficult period, remember Isaiah 43:2: "When you pass through the waters, I will be with you; and when you pass through the rivers, they will not sweep you over. When you walk through fire, you will not be burned." Saints reaffirm that when they sing "How Firm a Foundation!"

Alexander the Great, with all his conquests, with the known world as his footstool, cried out for another world to conquer. "A man's contentment is in his mind, not in the extent of his possessions. You say, 'If I had a little more, I should be very satisfied.' You make a mistake. If you are not content with what you have, you would not be satisfied if it were doubled."[40]

Is God and what he gives enough for you to be content? Or is his plan somehow defective? That may seem like a stark contrast, or even unfair, but it is in the final analysis quite consistent with what God says in his Word. God wants us to be content, not with what we have, but with what he gives. The next time you're tempted to grumble, stop, pause and ask: Has God failed to give me what he wills? Put the matter on his shoulders. Then be sensible enough to know that God is never mistaken, and then your calling as a Christian is to adjust. Ask God to help you be content with that.

Burroughs gives several tips on how to gain contentment:

1. If you would get a contented life, do not grasp too much of the world, or do not take in more of the business of the world than God calls you to.

2. Do not promise yourselves too much beforehand; do not reckon on too great things.

3. Labor to get your hearts mortified to the world, dead to the world.

4. Do not concentrate too much on afflictions.

5. Make a good interpretation of God's ways to you.

6. Do not be inordinately taken up with the comforts of this world when you have them.

After reading this work, the secret of contentment is better known. To practice its inculcation calls for enabling grace and persistence.

---

[40] *Spurgeon at His Best*, 41.

Chapter 8

Orthodoxy (Chesterton)

Luke 10:27-28; 1 Corinthians 11:16; Jude 3

Let me begin with a parable that I have written to support this chapter, *The Invasion from the Planet Hetero*

"It finally happened. They got their way. A great Revolution occurred in 2011, as the free thinkers of the planet Hetero took over earth. But the Revolution of Progress was not all it cracked up to be.

One of the first changes from the new administration was the radical alteration of the NFL, after settling the players' strike. Few politicians would dream of tampering with the age-old customs of the NFL, but under the rubric of alternative sports, Coach Harry Miles was soon unable to enjoy the once-great sport. Game times were changed to 3:00 AM on Tuesdays, and instead of pads and leather gear, the new NFL teams were outfitted with flowers and microphones. The flowers were the only protection given the players, so bone-crushing tackles disappeared. The microphones were part of the offensive arsenal. Under a new rule, whenever a player was about to be hit or tackled, he or she could automatically stop and read a verse of poetry. If that happened, the opposing player could not touch the poet, but had to sit down, hold the flowers which were handed off, and listen to the poem. And the worst rule of all was that in the 4th quarter, no matter how behind one team was, the loser would always be declared the winner. Only players with the most fumbles were selected for the Hall of Fame. Soon stadiums were empty, fans cared nothing for mediocrity, and the Union of College Elites heralded the new equality and demise of the former barbarism.

However, one pesky segment of society decided to unite and appeal to the new Hetero Supreme Court. They hired a sympathetic lawyer, prepared their briefs, and went to Cleveland—the new capital. Upon arrival at the Supreme Court, which met in an alley in a ghetto in Cleveland, the pro-NFL group looked for their briefcases and prepared to argue in court. They were shocked, however, when they learned that the Supreme Court consisted of 6 semi-pro Rap Musicians, 2 Cocaine smugglers, and 4 inmates from the closest prison. As the football plantiffs sought relief, they couldn't argue their case, amidst the boom boxes, the waning attention span of a crack-induced bench of judges, and the prisoners threw food at one another every time the football lawyers tried to make a point. The next day, the press reported the judicial branch proceedings as a triumph of the oppressed who were overthrowing patriarchy.

When the disappointed litigants left, they were ambushed and beaten. When the police were finally called, they only brought flowers. One of the attorneys recovered enough to call a cab to go to the Hospital. But the cab dropped the injured people off at the grocery store, telling them that instead of surgery, doctors now applied lettuce to any wound.

People were dying in the streets (which was called progress), buildings were trashed and the bricks given away as food, sanitation trucks hauled garbage into the art museums, and stop lights were put on a random computer program so that they never changed with the same frequency in any 24 hour period. Rush hour became crush hour. This was the land of Hetero."

I tell this little parable to illustrate what the world would be like if there was no such thing as orthodoxy—fixed or customary truth. *Hetero* is the Greek word for "other;" *ortho* is the word for correct. An orthodontist corrects teeth; an orthopedic surgeon corrects broken bones. Orthodoxy is correct teaching, and heterodoxy is deviation from true religious teaching. Some Christians have become phobic of orthodoxy without thinking about where things will lead if there is a truth vacuum.

In the parable above, as in true life, there are many areas in life that have their own orthodoxy. Without those correct versions, we do not merely have alternative routes, we have chaos. That is most true in the church. But before we get to that, let me restate something (in case the Parable was more confusing than clarifying):

Sports have their orthodoxies. There are rules and customs. Everyone does not always win. Some things are in bounds and other things are out of bounds. There are clear boundaries, stated rules, and expectations of conduct. These are all orthodoxies of sports. Without orthodoxy, athletics degenerates into chaos.

Law also has definite orthodoxies. If judges are not fair and do not apply the law, people who are harmed get hurt. In a court of law, certain codes of conduct, specific and unbending procedures, and legal principles carry the day. If courts devolve into therapy sessions or stages for multiculturalism, then justice disappears.

The same is true for medicine—one of the most important areas of our life. If doctors apply lettuce instead of surgery, we certainly would not receive much medical care. If orthodoxy is forsaken in medical care, all we have is alchemy or worse.

Nearly every area of life recognizes the concept of orthodoxy—whether it is as correct information, right practice, or standards of justice. Whatever your profession, there are certain standards required (frequently for licensing), and to go against those professional standards is to invite chaos. I could illustrate in many more areas, but you get the point.

So if people agree with this parable and my summary of how orthodoxy works in these areas, why do so many Christians react against the notion of biblical orthodoxy? Could it be that many have unwittingly become agents of heterodoxy? I think the main reason is because of a confusion. Many Christians confuse orthodoxy with a droll spiritual personna, but nothing could be further from the truth. Also, many Christians associate orthodoxy with old formalistic traditions, but neither is that necessarily so. Correct faith is the most lively, most adventuresome, most thrilling life possible. Orthodoxy is lively, energetic, and full. Don't confuse it with cheap imitations.

Orthodoxy is a good word. We want to be orthodox, not its opposite—heterodox. The Bible actually speaks a good deal about this. It makes some things plain and uses this word more often than some realize. Let's think about this a little more, and I also want to introduce you to a 20th century person who helped revive this vital concern.

Orthos in the NT

In the Gospels, a man was healed and when he started talking, he spoke correctly, plainly (Mk. 7:35). Jesus himself spoke of orthodoxy, using this root word in Lk. 7:43. In conversation with a Pharisee, when the Pharisee gave the correct answer, our Lord said, "You have judged correctly." On another occasion (Lk. 10:28), Jesus said to a lawyer, "You have answered orthodoxly." When his enemies tried to stump him near the end of his earthly ministry, when they were about to ask him how to pay taxes, they said, "Teacher we know that you speak and teach what is right . . ." (Lk. 20:21)

This term is also used or the concept alluded to in the NT Epistles.

Acts 2:42 is perhaps the earliest instance of orthodoxy, although the word is not used. In that verse we are informed that the early Christians immediately following Pentecost "devoted themselves to the apostles teaching and to the fellowship, to the breaking of bread and to prayer." These four items, apostolic doctrine, fellowship, the sacrament, and prayer, comprised the early orthodoxy. It was well-rounded and full. The Apostles teaching formed a set of theological truths that were not to be abandoned—no matter what a later age thought it discovered. These teachings were clear, known, and recognized as authoritative. The early church did not encourage each person to construe doctrine as each saw fit; nor did they expect that true Christians would despise the authoritative teachings of revelation.

By the time of Acts 16, the Council of Elders at Jerusalem settled a thorny doctrinal matter and even distributed its statement as a dogma (Acts 16:4). In Berea, the Christians were quite orthodox, as "they received the message with great eagerness and examined the Scriptures every day to see if what Paul said was true." Even Paul's teaching was subjected to the criteria of orthodoxy—which was revealed in God's Word.

Later, in Acts 20:27 the comprehensive system of truths is referred to as "the whole counsel of God."

The Book of Romans frequently alludes to orthodoxy. The opening verses speak about the "gospel God promised beforehand," and that gospel was fixed. It revolved around Jesus Christ being fully human and fully divine (Rom. 1:3-4). The remainder of that great epistle sets forth the orthodoxy we should believe.

1 and 2 Corinthians have several verses that mention the only view held by the church. For example, Paul writes the church and tells her not to associate with sexually immoral people (1 Cor. 5:9). In chapter 7 of that same epistle, Paul lays down principles for marriage, divorce, and commitment. He calls on Christians to persevere even in difficult relationships: "Nevertheless, each one should retain the place in life that the Lord assigned to him and to which God has called him. This is the RULE I lay down in all the churches." (1 Cor. 7:17). The rules or doctrines that were applicable to all churches formed the orthodoxy of the early church.

Paul would be surprised at the amount of relativism in many churches today. He does the same thing on the issue of the role of women in worship. After telling Christians that women are to be submissive in public worship (1 Cor. 11:3-13), he appeals to nature as teaching that it is disgraceful to confuse the roles assigned to males and females. (v. 14-15). He concludes that this is the only orthodox standard with these words: "If anyone wants to be contentious about this, we have no other practice—nor do the churches of God." Paul was fairly strong on this orthodoxy.

Likewise, he gave instructions on how to receive the Lord's Supper (1 Cor. 11:17-33), the gifts of the Spirit (1 Cor. 12), the Resurrection (ch. 15), and love (ch. 13). In several of these, he makes it clear that there is only one correct view. Note: orthodoxy applied not only to heady theological matters, but also to areas like the gifts of the Spirit, male-female relationships, and love. At the end of 1 Corinthians 14, Paul argued that the same standards were applicable "in all the congregations of the saints" (1 Cor. 14:34). If anyone differed with him on this, he rebuked: "Did the word of God originate with you? Or are you the only people it has reached." (v. 36). He called on the church to recognize a common and universal standard of faith and living. Even if a strong religious leader deviated from the fixed truth, "If he ignores this, he himself will be ignored." (14:38)

The point: There was one and only one view that came from God. Others might be rationalized, but God revealed one correct answer on the question at hand.

Philippians 3:15 called for mature Christians to agree on these matters: "If you think differently on some point, that too God will make clear to you." Paul believed that God would make the same truths known to all Christians. Sure, there would be minor differences, but if Christians live under God's Word, they have his promise that he will keep them in truth. As Jesus had prayed: "Sanctify them by thy Word; Thy Word is truth."

The Book of Ephesians is clear that one of the missions of the church is to uphold this revealed orthodoxy. God glorifies himself through the church (Eph. 3:21), that vehicle which often seems so frail to us. The church is elevated to a position of extreme prominence in 1 Timothy 3. First Timothy begins with Paul's command "not to teach false doctrine." (1 Tim. 1:3). That command assumes the notion of orthodoxy; how else could false doctrine be identified? Some had wandered away from the true faith (1:6) and taught that which was "contrary to the sound doctrine that conforms to the glorious gospel of the blessed God."

(1:10-11). The church is called God's household, but also is described in these lofty words: ". . . the church of the living God, the pillar and foundation of the truth." (1 Tim. 3:15). The church's organized and universally-held teaching is elevated to a level that is unchallenged by all other human thought. It is the pillar and ground of truth, because her only orthodoxy is the teaching given from the mind of God.

Several times, the letters to Timothy and Titus speak of "The" faith. In 1 Timothy 2:7 Paul described himself as a "teacher of the true faith." It is not just a "different strokes for different folks' faith." Deacons were to "keep hold of the deep truths of the faith with a clear conscience." (1 Tim. 3:9) It is "the faith" in numerous verses. Paul also spoke of "faithful sayings" which were small, widely recognized creedal type summations of truth. The early church was not afraid to set down what it believed and if necessary contend for it.

The qualifications for church officers make it clear that they were to hold to certain ideas and even oppose those who held others. Titus 1:9 specifies, "He must hold firmly to the trustworthy message as it has been taught, so that he can encourage others by sound doctrine and refute those who oppose it." Think of that whenever you choose your officers.

Hebrews 6:1-3 even records doctrines/practices that are said to be elementary. It is not necessary, that inspired book says, to "lay again the foundation of repentance from acts that lead to death, and of faith in God, instruction about baptisms, the laying on of hands, the resurrection of the dead, and eternal judgment." These things were considered orthodox, unamendable, and uniform for all Christians. Hebrews 12:13 exhorts us to strengthen our arms and legs, to make straight paths for our feet.

Concentrate briefly with me on the Book of Jude.

This short, one-chapter book was written by one who knew Jesus well. It is addressed to those "who have been called, who are loved by God the Father and kept by Jesus Christ." As a sharer of common salvation, Jude expressed his eagerness to urge his fellow Christians to "contend for the faith that was once for all entrusted to the saints." Three things should be noted about this verse. **First**, the faith is unchanging; it does not change over the centuries, nor depending on cultural or regional interests. It was handed down once and for all. It is not ongoing, it does not receive additional elements, nor are aspects of this faith to be subtracted. It is finished, and of a final nature. **Second**, it is handed down. The word is the word for tradition. Tradition actually means that which is handed on, or passed on with regularity. God intended this finished faith to be *traditioned*, handed down to successive generations. And according to this verse, he has entrusted that to the saints. All Christians, not only the officers, are to be involved in this baton-passing. **Third**, to do so recognizes the need to "contend for." It is possible to contend for the faith without being contentious. That is what God wants us to do. There are times when we have to energetically fight for the faith; we may even have to resist powerful trends and friends. The necessity of contending, however, is a small price to pay for orthodoxy.

Jude warned the first century Christians that some false teachers had slipped in. Although they appeared to be pious and appeared very mature, in reality, they were "godless men, who change the grace of God into a license for immorality and deny Jesus Christ our only Sovereign and Lord." (Jude 4). In that verse alone, we see that orthodoxy must be zealously guarded and that vigilance is called for. The fault-lines of heretical teaching are even alluded to in this verse. These heretics pervert grace into immorality. That is one sign of heterodoxy: if you see a teacher's disciples gravitating toward immorality—regardless of the interpretation placed on it— BEWARE. Two specific doctrinal articles are mentioned in v. 4. Orthodoxy champions Jesus Christ as our unique Sovereign and as Lord. Both of these were critical at the writing of Jude, and since the faith is unchanged, must be critical still. We must contend for the sovereignty of Jesus Christ, not the will of man; and we must adhere with all that we have to his divine Lordship. He is the boss—not human beings or organizations.

God had, according to Jude, a history of destroying unbelievers and false teachers (v. 5). He even cast out the fallen angels when they abandoned his orthodoxy. In fact, that may be a key to understanding orthodoxy. It is God's not our's. After the Reformation, a theological phrase (in Latin) arose: *"One cannot give that which is not his to give."* Salvation is not ours to dispense, hence we must not act as if we can. Similarly, sovereign power comes from God, and his church can only dispense what he gives her. Likewise, orthodoxy is not ours to be created, tailored, or even polished. It is God's and not ours to give. Therefore, we can/should attend to it, support it, proclaim it, and study it. But we cannot give it nor amend it. It is the Sovereign Lord's orthodoxy. The only thing we create is heterodoxy.

Here's how Jude concludes about those who would pervert the doctrine God reveals: "Woe to them! They have taken the way of Cain; they have rushed for profit into Balaam's error; they have been destroyed in Korah's rebellion. These men are blemishes at your love feasts, eating with you without the slightest qualm—shepherds who feed only themselves. They are clouds without rain, blown among by the wind; autumn trees, without fruit and uprooted—twice dead. They are wild waves of the sea, foaming up their shame; wandering stars, for whom blackest darkness has been reserved forever." God does not think too highly of un-orthodoxy.

Michael Green wrote: "Apostolic teaching, not whatever be the current theological fashion, is the hallmark of authentic Christianity. The once-for-allness of the apostolic faith is inescapably bound up with the particularity of the incarnation, in which God spoke to men through Jesus once and for all. And simply because Christianity is a historical religion, the witness of the original hearers . . . is determinative of what we can know about Jesus." (loc. cit, p. 159)

If you're not already familiar with a great Christian writer, you should become familiar with G. K. Chesterton. Many of you know who C. S. Lewis was and what a great Christian apologist he was in the mid-20th century. He counted Chesterton as one of his mentors. Gilbert Keith Chesterton was born in Kensington England in May of 1874. A witty and well-educated child, his parents recognized his artistic ability, and enrolled him in the Slade School of Art.[41] Upon

---

[41] This biographical section taken from my (1995) *The Arrogance of the*

completion of his work there, his earliest successes in life were as an illustrator. His teenage years coincided with the arrival of humanistic skepticism in England at the turn of the century. He was exposed to all the 'modern' notions associated with unbelief.

In 1901, he married Frances Bogg who introduced him to the Anglican Church. His subsequent pilgrimage toward Orthodoxy was a colorful one.

He began writing at a young age, and soon was published as a novelist, a poet, a literary critic, a playwright, an editor, and eventually as serious essayist. The topics he addressed were broad and he frequently exhibited a style that was refreshingly irreverent. The author of *The Napoleon of Notting Hill* (a book of political fiction), *Heretics* (an expose' of the errors of major philosophical schools at the time), and *What's Wrong with the World* (a social critique), he also wrote literary critiques of the works of Robert Browning and Charles Dickens. Chesterton was one of the most literary of Christians in the 20th century. In addition, he would become known for his published studies on *St. Thomas Aquinas* and *St. Francis of Assisi*. Two of his most enduring works were: *The Everlasting Man* and his *Autobiography* that documented his trek into the Roman Catholic Church.

He provides a testimonial to his conversion away from modernity and its notions in his return back to ancient orthodoxy. Listen in.

> It was as if I had been blundering about since my birth with two huge and unmanageable machines, of different shapes and without apparent connection—the world and the Christian tradition. I had found this hole in the world: the fact that one must somehow find a way of loving the world without trusting it; somehow one must love the world without being worldly. I found this projecting feature of Christian theology, like a sort of hard spike, the dogmatic insistence that God was personal, and had made a world separate from himself. The spike of dogma fitted exactly into the hole in the world—it had evidently been meant to go there—and then the strange thing began to happen. When once

Modern.

these two parts of the two machines had come together, one after another, all the other parts fitted and fell in with an eerie exactitude. I could hear bolt after bolt over all the machinery falling into its place with a kind of click of relief. Having got one part right, all the other parts were repeating that rectitude, as clock after clock strikes noon. Instinct after instinct was answered by doctrine after doctrine. Or, to vary the metaphor, I was like one who had advanced into a hostile country to take one high fortress. And when that fort had fallen the whole country surrendered and turned solid behind me. The whole land was lit up, as it were, back to the first fields of my childhood. All those blind fancies of boyhood . . . became suddenly transparent and sane.[42]

His profession of coming to orthodoxy needs to be heard in part.

I was a pagan at the age of twelve, and a complete agnostic by the age of sixteen; I read the scientific and skeptical literature of my time . . . I never read a line of Christian apologetics. I read as little as I can of them now. It was Huxley and Herbert Spencer and Bradlaugh who brought me back to orthodox theology. They sowed in my mind my first wild doubts of doubt. Our grandmothers were quite right when they said that Tom Paine and the freethinkers unsettled the mind. They do. They unsettled mine horribly. The rationalist made me question whether reason was of any use whatever; and when I had finished Herbert Spencer I had got as far as doubting (for the first time) whether evolution had occurred at all. As I laid down the last of Colonel Ingersoll's atheistic lectures the dreadful thought broke across my mind, 'Almost thou persuadest me to be a Christian.' I was in a desperate way. (84)

Chesterton reported this "odd effect of the great agnostics in arousing doubts deeper than their own might be illustrated in many ways. . . . As I read and re-read all the non-Christian or anti-Christian accounts of the faith, from Huxley to Bradlaugh, a slow and awful impression grew gradually but graphically upon my mind,

---

[42] G. K. Chesterton, *Orthodoxy* (New York: Doubleday, 1990), 153. The page numbers in parentheses are to this edition until otherwise noted.

the impression that Christianity must be a most extraordinary thing. For not only (as I understood) had Christianity the most flaming vices, but it had apparently a mystical talent for combining vices which seemed inconsistent with each other. It was attacked on all sides and for all contradictory reasons." (84)

In 1922, he was received into the Roman Catholic Church under the ministry of Father John O'Connor (who was the model for Father Brown in Chesterton's series of detective novels). His writings leave a trail of one who went from an ardent agnostic to a strong, quite traditional believer. His 1908 book *Orthodoxy* (a most eloquent book, written when he was only thirty four) attempts to answer his critics who thought he was flirting with insanity for professing his faith. This book was intended to be a companion to his *Heretics*; in it he sought to positively state what he believed in contrast to the critique contained in *Heretics*. Chesterton saw Orthodoxy as an explanation "not of whether the Christian faith can be believed, but of how [he] personally came to believe it. The book is therefore arranged upon the positive principle of a riddle and its answer. It deals first with all the writer's own solitary and sincere speculations and then with all the startling style in which they were all suddenly satisfied by the Christian Theology." (vi)

Chesterton died on June 14, 1936, a stalwart defender of orthodoxy and a literate apologist for the Christian faith. His work (69 books while he was alive, with an additional 10 posthumous works) and approach are worthy of acquaintance.

Let me acquaint you with a few of his excellent thoughts to encourage you in the pursuit of orthodoxy.

Of the embarrassment of thinking that he had discovered something brand new, Chesterton confessed: "As usual, I found that Christianity had been there before me. The whole history of my Utopia has the same amusing sadness. I was always rushing out of my architectural study with plans for a new turret only to find it sitting up there in the sunlight, shining, and a thousand years old. . . . Without vanity, I really think there was a moment when I could have invented the marriage vow (as an institution) out of my own head; but I discovered, with a sigh, that it had been invented already." (122)

Nearly a century earlier, G. K. Chesterton gave testimony about the value of rediscovering our past Christian heritage, when he found that the best truths had already been mined:

> I did, like all other solemn little boys, try to be in advance of the age. Like them I tried to be some ten minutes in advance of the truth. And I found that I was eighteen hundred years behind it . . . When I fancied that I stood alone I was really in the ridiculous position of being backed up by all Christendom. It may be, Heaven forgive me, that I did try to be original; but I only succeeded in inventing all by myself an inferior copy of the existing traditions of civilized religion . . . It might amuse a friend or an enemy to read how I gradually learnt from the truth of some stray legend or from the falsehood of some dominant philosophy, things that I might have learnt from my catechism—if I had ever learnt it . . . I found at last what I might have found in the nearest parish church.

Chesterton was particularly disdainful toward the modernization of theology: "Now let us take in order the innovations that are the notes of the new theology or the modernist church. . . . The very doctrine which is called the most old-fashioned was found to be the only safeguard of the new democracies of the earth. The doctrine seemingly most unpopular was found to be the only strength of the people.

He sounds like Lord Acton who asked, "How is man superior to prejudice, passion, and interest?" His answer: "By the study of History and the pursuit of the required character." Moreover, he recommended an option that is often ignored: "Resist your time—take a foothold outside it—see other times and ask yourself whether the time of our ancestors is fit for us."

Chesterton taught that orthodoxy was like a white fence post. Unfortunately, many people think that the way to conserve certain things is to leave them alone. Chesterton, however, was more realistic. He said that if you leave a fence-post alone, it does not stay white; it becomes old, dirty, and rotten. The only way to keep a fence-post white is to re-apply a fresh coat of paint regularly. That is true in terms of orthodoxy: we must re-apply the ancient truths, not ignore them.

Following his conversion away from the sloppiness of non-Christian thought, Chesterton became an advocate of doctrinal precision. To the "modern critics of the history of Christianity," the "monstrous wars about small points of theology, the earthquakes of emotion about a gesture or a word" were inexplicable. Of the narrow margin between orthodoxy and heresy, Chesterton explained:

> It was only a matter of an inch; but an inch is everything when you are balancing. The Church could not afford to swerve a hair's breadth on some things if she was to continue her great and daring experiment of the irregular equilibrium. Once let one idea become less powerful and some other idea would become too powerful. (100)

What should you do to embrace orthodoxy?

1. Do your own study. All people are not called to be professional theologians, yet every Christian needs to know a little about what true Christianity is. If you have never done a study of what elements are essential to Christianity, do so as soon as possible. Books are available in church libraries, or pastors/elders are happy to assist you. Do one study in the coming year.
2. Listen around you. Today, you will find many ideas that do not match up with Scripture. Learn to dissect some of those errors and don't fall for them. Fathers and mothers especially should take time to know these, so they can assist their children in avoiding errors.
3. Look for this in officers and ministers. The local church is the first line of orthodoxy; if it crumbles so will other institutions. Give it your first effort.
4. Give some of your time in the coming year to help spread this orthodoxy. Some may do it with computers, others with sound teaching, or still others in the community, school, or

home. Wherever you live and in whatever the realm that God allows you to reach, do it for orthodoxy.

5. Be thankful if your are in a church where orthodoxy is valued.

Here's a concluding question: Can orthodoxy be overdone? Can it squeeze the life out of true spirituality?

Consider the Pharisees. They are often held up as people not to imitate. I certainly agree with that: Don't imitate the Pharisees. But the Pharisees were not bad because of their orthodoxy. What makes them so bad is the opposite: they did not hold to nor practice the kind of spirituality that God intended. They had created their own little system of legalism. They had misinterpreted the promises of God. Their problem was not that they overdid orthodoxy; no, they were off the track altogether. They had deviated from the correct path of God's teaching and were in the process of creating their own religion—the religion of Judaism, complete with its assumption of ethnic superiority.

If one correctly understands God's Word it leads to a balanced, well-rounded, full life. Real orthodoxy does not concentrate on doctrine alone, but all of life. Along with a strongly orthodox embrace of divine election comes also a zeal for evangelism. Side by side with biblical views that each person is responsible for his own family's welfare is also the clear teaching that the church should extend mercy and concrete support whenever possible. These are all matters of biblical orthodoxy. Orthodoxy does not apply only to one's head, but also to one's heart. In fact, when God's Word is most truly understood, it will inevitably lead to an emotional response that is in keeping with orthodoxy. That's why God said: "Love the Lord your God with all your heart, soul, mind, and strength."

That's orthodox.

Chapter 9

Mere Christianity (C. S. Lewis)

Acts 2:42 and 20:27; Deuteronomy 6:4; Matthew 22:34-40

Let me begin with both a challenge and a summation of my chapter: "For the remainder of this year, will you join me in living and pursuing "Mere Christianity"? I thought I'd begin with a moderate challenge instead of a herculean one. The challenge, using the title of one of C. S. Lewis' most famous books, is not to exceed normal Christianity, but simply to come up to the standard. Actually, as C. S. Lewis admitted, this phrase originated with Richard Baxter, a 17th century Puritan, who preached in London. Baxter described it as plain Christianity, one without frills.

So often, we attend an inspirational conference, or hear a stirring sermon, or we're challenged by some provocative idea. We set our goals high when we hear such ideas, and then our lives resume and we find ourselves not living up to expectations, or even falling down. It is frustrating to fail to meet our own targets.

So in this chapter, I want to urge you to set your sights a little lower, but also to have them set on the right target, and also to hit the target. Think with me, if you haven't in a while about "Mere Christianity."

Clive Staples Lewis (1898-1963) was a novelist, poet, and apologist who was born in Belfast. He was an Anglican layman who taught at both Oxford and Cambridge, "and attracted wide readership during and after WW II because he had, "the rare gift of making righteousness readable."[43] He burst on the scene in 1941 with the clever satire *Screwtape Letters*—instructions from a senior devil to a junior devil on how to snatch a new Christian from the snares of heaven. Soon after (1943), Lewis delivered a series of twenty-nine widely popular broadcast talks on basic Christian doctrine. They were, like Lewis's later writings, biblical wake-up calls; he avoided denominational distinctives and called it "mere Christianity." The stamp of his style was wit, clarity, an effortless elegance, and disciplined logic.

In scholarly circles Lewis was a respected literary critic before *Screwtape* surfaced. Books flowed from his pen at the rate of one or more a year, and in astonishing variety: novels, children's books, theology, philosophical apologetics, poetry, literary criticism. Many of his books seemed especially designed to remove obstacles facing the Christian in an agnostic age of scientific materialism. *The Abolition of Man* (1943), on the rational and social necessity of a normative ethic, and *Miracles* (1947), a philosophical defense of the possibility of miracles, were closely reasoned philosophical treatises. *The Problem of Pain* (1940) dealt with the ancient difficulty of justifying the ways of a good God to suffering man. *Reflections on the Psalms* (1958) and *Letters to Malcolm: Chiefly on Prayer* (1963) discussed problems in the Psalms, prayer, and the private devotional life. His three most popular novels, *Out of the Silent Planet* (1938), *Perelandra* (1943), and *That Hideous Strength* (1945), wove Christianity into a hauntingly beautiful fictionalized cosmic myth. The seven *Chronicles of Narnia* became modern children's classics.

---

[43] The biographical sketch in this chapter is taken from J. D. Douglas, ed., *The New International Dictionary of the Christian Church* (Grand Rapids: Zondervan, 1979), 593-594. Others in this volume abbreviated by NIDCC are also taken from that standard dictionary.

C. S. Lewis disliked "chronological snobbery," the notion that newest is best. . . . He believed myths were based on something real, and that Christianity had an objective correlative.

Lewis became an atheist as a teenage schoolboy. His education at Oxford was interrupted by military service in World War I. After recovery from a shell wound he returned to Oxford to teach English literature. After nearly thirty years as fellow of Magdalen College, he left Oxford in 1954 for the newly created chair of medieval and Renaissance English at Cambridge. Lewis moved slowly from atheism through Yeatsian romanticism to absolute idealism and finally theism, returning to worship in the Church of England in 1929. His conversion journey is traced in *The Pilgrim's Regress* (1933), an allegory, and *Surprised by Joy* (1955), his spiritual autobiography. Most of his life was spent in quiet bachelorhood, but in 1956 he married Joy Davidman Gresham, an American Jewish Christian convert, when she was critically ill with cancer. After her death in 1960 he wrote the poignant *A Grief Observed*, initially published under a pseudonym." When it is all over and done with, C. S. Lewis may be the major Apologist of 20th century.

The Bible depicts mere Christianity several times in its pages. For example, Acts 2:42 describes how the earliest Christians were united in the apostolic teaching, the sacrament, fellowship, and prayer. Indeed, these are four constituent elements of true Christianity. Anything less is sub-Christian. Earlier in the Gospels, the disciples of Jesus intimated that there was one true and only Christianity when they rhetorically queried: "Lord to whom else shall we go for the words of eternal life." (Jn. 6:66)

This is also one of the best selling and most influential books in our time. You might do well to be familiar with its theme or contents. It is well worth purchasing for about the price of two Super-Value meals at McDonald's.

Throughout, I want to contrast Mere Christianity first of all with Super Christianity. Super means above ordinary. This is hyper-Christianity, or the call for elements of Christianity that may not be normal. There are times of intensity in our faith; there are also times of normalcy. Most people cannot zoom through life at the speed of a

100 yard dash. They may train differently for a Marathon. Spirituality is not so much a constant sprint as it is a constant drive. I cannot call on you to be herculean Christians, but any Pastor would be most satisfied with a congregation of mere Christians.

However, many congregations consist of **sub-Christianity**.

Sub-Christianity is that which falls below the norms of Scripture. It does not live up to its calling. Whether due to a combination of worldliness, or because of lack of teaching, or whatever, sub-Christianity is man's attempt to have his spiritual cake and eat it, too. It is the human attempt to keep one hand on the world and one hand in heaven, and that won't work. Sub-Christianity seeks to find the minimums of Christianity and push those yet lower. I'll be satisfied with Mere Christianity.

Many different statistical studies reveal about 80% of Americans view themselves as Theists. Recently, a Barna survey noted that less than 20% of Americans believe in both God and the Bible, & less than 10% have a biblical world view. However, if you ask a visitor to our country, "Does this look like a place where 80% believe in God and 20% are evangelicals, that visitor might not affirm that he sees much Christianity. The reality is that many who profess Christianity, not only do not live up to super Christianity, they don't live up to Mere Christianity. As a result, Sub Christianity prevails in many sectors.

Ask why? I can think of three reasons.

1) A misunderstanding of conversion: Many think of conversion in terms of an outward experience or momentary surge of emotions. Some think that one should have a single conversion "experience," and that thereafter, everything else may stay the same. That is a grave misunderstanding of new life. Still some focus on a particular experience, and once that experience is had, they forget the rest. That is sub-Christianity. Mere Christianity presents conversion as an entire and massive change in life and values.

Related to this is a second possible culprit:

2) A confusion perpetuated by many evangelicals: Some believe that a person can pray to receive Christ as Savior, but only later

embrace him as Lord. They may think of themselves as preaching Grace Alone, but they are also distorting the teaching of Scripture, turning grace into something else. Christ does not come to a sinner as a Divine Beggar. He comes as Lord, gently but also with all power. If he is not Lord of one's life, then who is? The answer may not lead to Mere Christianity but to Mere Humanism.

3) Lack of internal standards within the church for her own leadership or absence of church discipline. Sub-Christianity nearly always results when standards are not held high, or when leaders compromise them. Sinners, or even the saints, will not always behave well on an honor system. We need others around us to encourage us to do what God wants us to. When accountability and discipline are lost inside the church, sub-Christianity results.

The Scripture describes Mere Christianity in several places. In the Book of Acts 11:26, believers are for the first time called "Christians" in Antioch, because there they were associated with Christ. The word Christian means, little Christ. It describes one who follows or imitates Christ. Interestingly, if you think about it, being a Christian does not require leadership. It requires follower-ship. Everywhere we look, we see that Christians follow Christ, they imitate Christ, they submit to him, and do what he asks. 3rd membership vow!! They are not asked to be superstars, nor to invent or create a new religion. We are to be subservient, and merely live up to what he says.

That's the **first** aspect of Mere Christianity that you should seek to cultivate: *followership*. Imitate Christ.

Second, Mere Christianity is that Christianity that is true in any century, not just today with all of the fads that become tomorrow's laughable foibles.

Lewis: describes 'mere' Christianity as "what it is and was, what it was long before I was born and whether I like it or not."[44] It may

---

[44] C. S. Lewis, *Mere Christianity*, Christian Library Edition {Westwood, NJ: Barbour and Company, Inc., 1952), preface. All references in parentheses to this edition.

clarify what Mere Christianity is, if we apply this standard of timelessness to it. That is to say, if it is an emphasis only for a time, season, or area, then it may not be at the heart of Mere Christianity. Mere Christianity transcends time and place. For example, when I was a young Christian, it was imperative (so we were told) to witness every day or read our Bible 20 minutes per day. That may be too narrow.

Similarly, belief in the Second Coming in conjunction with certain events in Israel is not Mere Christianity, if tied too closely to our time and place. Mere Christianity embraces the biblical teaching that Christ will return, and that he will return gloriously, visibly, and with the self-same body from his resurrection. There are many truths affirmed by Scripture about the end-times. These form part of Mere Christianity. However, there are some end-time schemes that actually call for 'going beyond' or extra-Christianity. I cannot honestly call on you to live up to those.

If one asks, "Aren't you reducing this to the Apostles' Creed only?" let me give two responses.

(1) No, I do not believe the Apostles Creed is the only safe statement of faith. I believe the Scriptures teach a number of things that go beyond that. The Apostles Creed is great, it is wonderful to unite the Trinitarian faith, but we also believe in the "whole counsel" of God (Acts 20:27). Look at that verse for a moment with me. I would not call you to Mere Christianity that is reduced Christianity. I want to call you only to that—and to all that—which is scriptural. To allow you to go home satisfied only to keep the "half counsel" of God is to encourage you to follow Sub-Christianity. I want to call you to meet the standard, only the right standard.

Acts 20:27 tells us that Paul declared to the church "the whole counsel of God," not the scaled-down version. The early preachers and missionaries were intent on expounding all God's revelation, all his will, the whole counsel. You should desire that today, and recognize that as part of Mere Christianity.

I cannot call on you to live up to "slight" Christianity; that is not what this is. Rather, we are called to live up to the highest possible revelation of Christ. The Apostles Creed is not the end of Christianity but the beginning.

(**Third**) Mere Christianity is full, robust, well-rounded Christianity. It is living fully, to the fullest information God has given us.

(2) On the other hand, there are some who don't even live up to the Creed. There are theologians who deny the virgin birth and the historical resurrection. It would be a definite improvement if they were to live up to the Christian basics contained in the Apostles Creed. There are also some professing Christians in the pew who do not believe in creation, and many don't believe in the forgiveness of sins or the resurrection of the body. I don't believe the Apostles Creed is the end-all for Christianity in our day. However, it would be progress if some believed in it. Target the creed as your bare minimum; Mere Christianity-lite. But there is much more that God has revealed for us.

A **fourth** aspect of Mere Christianity for Lewis was the notion that there were universal laws of morality. Lewis makes two preliminary points: "First, that human beings, all over the earth, have this curious idea that they ought to behave in a certain way, and cannot really get rid of it. Secondly, that they do not in fact behave in that way. They know the Law of Nature; they break it. These two facts are the foundation of all clear thinking about ourselves and the universe we live in." (7)

Lewis thought that certain things were true anywhere. I agree. He challenged, "Think of a country where people were admired for running away in battle, or where a man felt proud of double-crossing all the people who had been kindest to him. You might just as well try to imagine a country where *two and two made five*. Men have differed as regards what people you ought to be unselfish to— whether it was only your own family, or your fellow countrymen, or everyone. But they have always agreed that you ought not to put yourself first. Selfishness has never been admired." He added, "Men have differed as to whether you should have one wife or four. But they have always agreed that you must not simply have any woman you liked." (5-6). He rightly noted, to a world that was slipping in terms of basic morality, that God's law is applicable in all cultures and at all times. Those features that are continually true comprise Mere Christianity. Mere Christianity believes in the moral law.

Lewis pointed out eloquently: "But the most remarkable thing is this. Whenever you find a man who says he does not believe in a real Right and Wrong, you will find the same man going back on this a moment later. He may break his promise to you, but if you try breaking one to him he will be complaining, 'It's not fair' before you can saw Jack Robinson. A nation may say treaties do not matter, but then next minute, they spoil their case by saying that the particular treaty they want to break was an unfair one. But if treaties do not matter, and if there is no such thing as Right and Wrong—in other words, if there is no Law of Nature—what is the difference between a fair treaty and an unfair one? Have they not let the cat out of the bag and shown that, whatever they say, they really know the Law of Nature just like anyone else?" (6)

C. S. Lewis did the church a large favor by pointing out that "we have failed to practice ourselves the kind of behavior we expect from other people." (6). Thus, the Golden Rule is still applicable. I sincerely believe that our witness as a church could be greatly enhanced if we lived by the Golden Rule. Of course, it takes God's animating grace living in us to do this. For example, when you go to the store, and are undercharged, what do you do?

Mere Christianity—not super Christianity—remembers the standards of God and puts them into practice, even if it is not to our advantage. A merely Christian owner will not steal from his customer; if his product is defective, he won't wrangle or steal, but will treat his neighbor like himself. A mere Christian nurse or doctor will practice the Golden Rule in taking shifts and in caring for others. A mere Christian teacher will treat students as she wants her own children treated. A mere Christian worker will work as unto the Lord. This is not super-Christianity, but true Christianity.

Similarly, when you are in the coffee-break room, and the other colleagues begin to trash someone's reputation. Do you ask, "How does 'Do unto others as you would have others do unto you' apply to this situation?" Or is it OK for you to lust after someone else's wife, but not for someone to leer at your own? How about those duties to our neighbor? The true Christian accepts them as responsibilities from God.

A **fifth** aspect of Mere Christianity is moral living after conversion.

A **sixth** essential aspect of Mere Christianity is repentance. As Lewis and others point out, Christianity may not make sense until we first understand something about "Why" we need Christ. To fail to see the need for Christ, as required by the Moral Law, is a mistake. "Christianity simply does not make sense until you have faced the sort of facts I have been describing. Christianity tells people to repent and promises them forgiveness. It therefore has nothing . . . to say to people who do not know they have done anything to repent of and who do not feel that they need any forgiveness." (27). As soon as you realize that you have broken the law and stand in condemnation without some acquittal, "it is after all this, and not a moment sooner, that Christianity begins to talk." (27)

These facts of Mere Christianity are "terrifying facts." (27) "I wish," said Lewis, "it was possible to say something more agreeable. But I must say . . . that the Christian religion . . . does not begin in comfort; it begins in the dismay I have been describing, and it is no use at all trying to go on to that comfort without first going through that dismay. In religion, as in war and everything else, comfort is the one thing you cannot get by looking for it. If you look for truth, you may find comfort in the end; if you look for comfort you will not get either comfort or truth—only soft soap and wishful thinking to begin with and, in the end, despair. Most of us have got over the pre-war wishful thinking about politics. It is time we did the same with religion." (27-28)

Seventh: Mere Christianity also requires an adherence to absolute truth. "Being a Christian does mean thinking that where Christianity differs from other religions, Christianity is right and they are wrong. As in arithmetic—there is only one right answer to a sum, and all other answers are wrong." (31) Christianity does not agree with relativism or perspective-ism. It supports absolutes.

Eighth: Belief in the reality of sin and devil. Mere Christianity also involves "The Shocking Alternative." "Christians, then believe that an evil power has made himself for the present the Prince of this World." (41). The reality of Satan, unfortunately is part of orthodox Christianity. Lewis calls this the "Dark Power." From a cosmic point of view, Lewis observed: "Terrific energy is expended—civilizations are built up—excellent institutions devised; but each time something goes wrong. Some fatal flaw always brings the selfish cruel people to the top and it all slides back into misery and ruin. In fact, the machine conks. It seems to start up all right and runs a few yards, and then it breaks down. They are trying to run it on the wrong juice. That is what Satan has done to us humans." (43-44) To continually remind us, however, that we live in a fallen universe, Lewis summarized three antidotes. First, God gave a conscience to all men to remind them of the better. Second, he gives good dreams—some of those odd stories about a god who dies and comes to life again. Third, he "selected one particular people and spent several centuries hammering into their heads the sort of God he was—that there was only one of him and that he care about right conduct." (44)

This is the famous backdrop for Lewis' Grand Trilemma. You may have heard it alluded to or described. If not, it is too good to resist reviewing. Amidst these good dreams comes a shock. Suddenly, one of these Jewish men claims to forgive sins and says that he always existed. Further, he claims that he will return to judge the world at the end of time. That's all. However, the claim to forgive sins is so preposterous as to be absurd, comic, or true. Jesus had the nerve to tell people their sins were forgiven. He never had to consult someone first, or check in with some other religious authority. "He unhesitatingly behaved as if he was the party chiefly concerned, the person chiefly offended in all offenses. This makes sense only if he really was the God whose laws are broken and whose love is wounded in every sin. In the mouth of any speaker who is not God, these words would imply what I can only regard as

a silliness and conceit unrivaled by any other character in history."
(45) Yet, even his enemies did not regard him as silly or conceited.
They at least took him as a serious threat. So much so that they had
to kill him.

It is not, therefore, appropriate argued Lewis to merely buss
Jesus as a great moral teacher. "That is one thing we must not say. A
man who was merely a man and said the sort of things Jesus said
would not be a great moral teacher. He would either be a lunatic—
on a level with a man who says he is a poached egg—or else he
would be the Devil of Hell. You must make your choice. Either this
man was, and is, the Son of God: or else a madman or something
worse. You can shut him up for a fool, you can spit at him and kill
him as a demon; or you can fall at his feet and call him Lord and
God. But let us not come with any patronizing nonsense about his
being a great human teacher. He had not left that open to us. He did
not intend to." (45)

So, the question lies before us that Jesus himself asked centuries
ago: "Who do you say that I am?" What about you? Do you believe
Jesus to be the Lord of all—not only the wisest and the best, but also
God in the flesh? Who lives inside the heart and mind of every
believer? And do you believe that in more places than this sanctuary
and at more times than on Sunday?

Below I summarize the essential aspects of Mere Christianity:

1. followership. Imitate Christ.
2. true in any century.
3. full, robust, well-rounded Christianity. It is living fully, to the
fullest information God has given us.
4. universal laws of morality exist.
5. moral living after conversion.
6. repentance.
7. requires an adherence to absolute truth.
8. Believe in the reality of sin and devil.
9. Accepts Christ as who he claimed to be.

Mere Christianity; it is not new. It dates back to the oldest of times. Moses expressed it this way: "The Lord our God is one. Love the Lord your God with all your heart and with all your soul and with all your strength."

And then in the NT, Jesus reiterated it: When asked what was the greatest commandment, Jesus narrowed it down to the essence of Mere Christianity. He said that the greatest commandment was the same one that Moses had given. "Love the Lord your God with all your heart and with all your soul and with all your mind." (Mt. 22:37). He also added to that, "And love your neighbor as yourself." For Jesus, "all the Law and the Prophets hung on those to duties. That was mere Christianity. Later in the NT, Paul said it this way: "If you confess with your mouth, 'Jesus is Lord,' and believe in your heart that God raised him from the dead, you will be saved." (Rom. 10:9)

James described it: "Pure and undefiled religion is this: to look after orphans and widows in their distress and to keep oneself from being polluted by the world." (Jas. 1:27). In the verse before, he had taught that the supreme test of one's spirituality is the control of the tongue. This is mere Christianity. Mere Christianity always unites faith and action.

It may be described in many different ways, but however one bundles it, Mere Christianity amounts to this: a full-souled love for and service to Jesus Christ. The Mere Christian knows that life is dead without Jesus. The Mere Christian knows that he is a sinner, unable to save himself or to drastically improve the world without supernatural help. The Mere Christian throws himself to the mercy of God, trusting in Jesus alone to get him out of this mess we call sin, and thereafter to guide, protect, and sustain life here and after death. To be sure, that has the tendency to mightily change one's life. It should. Mere Christianity produces fruit that lasts.

Mere Christianity is that life of faith that has transformed millions and that which has satisfied millions more. But don't choose it because of its practical efficacy. Choose it only because you have a gnawing sense that—imperfect though you be—God has chosen you. Indeed, he chose to send Jesus, the perfect Lamb of God to die for you.

One of the most influential Christians in our time is Watergate convict, Charles Colson. He read this book by C. S. Lewis at his own personal low ebb during the final days of the Watergate hearings. He tells of visiting a friend, a President of a very large business. A great success, this man astonished Colson during the visit. Colson had arranged the visit to see if he had any ways out. Upon arriving, however, he found a changed man. When Colson asked the Executive what was different, the man told him that he had accepted Jesus Christ as his Lord. Colson was shocked, but could not repudiate the obvious change in priorities and lifestyle. Colson was intrigued and began to see his own life as bankrupt, and this man gave him a small book by a British scholar entitled *Mere Christianity*. Colson began with a chapter on "Pride," was cut to the heart, and realized that pride was a spiritual cancer. Listen to how God has used this book for Colson and many others.[45]

"The events of my own life flashed before me. I thought I had been driven by a desire to provide for my family, build a good law firm, serve my country. But in reality what I was doing all those years was feeding my pride, proving how good I was. Lewis convicted me that all my efforts have been in vain, that in my drive for the top I had missed the real pinnacle—to know God in a personal way.

As I left my friend's home that night, I accepted his gift of the copy of *Mere Christianity*. I was deeply moved by his testimony and by the chapter he had read—though I refused to show it. But as I got into my car, the White House tough guy—the hatchet man, or so the press called me—crumbled in a flood of tears, unable to drive, calling out to God with the first honest prayer of my life. That was the night Jesus Christ came into my life.

Over the next week, I read the book as if I was studying for the most important case I had ever argued. Lewis' logic was so utterly compelling that I was left with no recourse but to accept the reality of the God who is and who has revealed himself through Jesus Christ. *Mere Christianity* simply sets forth a powerful, rational case

---

[45] For Colson's own full account of his conversion, see his *Born Again* (Old Tappan, NJ: Chosen Books,1976), 109-117.

for the Christian faith in a wonderfully readable way. Since then I have given out hundreds of copies of *Mere Christianity* and have met thousands whose lives have been transformed by it." Other than the Bible, God has used this book most powerfully in my life.

But I must warn you, it is not a book [nor is the Bible!] you can pick up and put down easily, nor is it a book you can read and return to being the same person you were before. For it masterfully presents the case for Christ. After reading it, the uncommitted person can only make a choice for or against him.

Let me close with this quote from an earlier preacher who also understood Mere Christianity, Daniel Cawdry: "Christ came not to possess our brains with some cold opinions that send down a freezing and benumbing influence into our hearts. Christ was a master of the life, not of the school; and he is the best Christian whose heart beats with the purest pulse towards heaven, not he whose head spins the finest cobweb."

Mere Christianity. Will you commit yourself to this in the future? If you will, you will never turn back. Love him merely and sincerely from this day forward.

Chapter 10

Charles Spurgeon: *All of Grace*

Ephesians 2:8-9

In a previous chapter, we discussed the 'bondage of the will.' We saw the orthodox Christian teaching that even the best of humans were/are bound by human limitations. The human will is seldom a solution to a real problem. So, we might ask: How can we make it in life and into eternity? My answer is the same for both: Only By God's Strong Grace. In this chapter, I hope to devote my comments to that subject.

There is, however, an even narrower question: Do we make it in life partially by grace or totally by grace? To ask the question in terms of a great classic by Baptist pastor Charles Spurgeon, is Christian living "All of Grace"?

Partially by Grace?

I'm afraid that all too many modern Christians act as if we live life "partially by grace." These religious people (Maybe you'll recognize someone you know or even yourself in what follows) believe something like this: "Sure, we are all a little sinful. But still, we have some merit in us. We should turn to Christ for salvation, but remember this motto: 'God helps those who help themselves.' (That's NOT in the Bible)." Then after turning to Christ, these people believe in prayer (partially), in sacrifice (a little), in obedience to the Lord (unless it becomes extreme), and when times are difficult, we are to depend on God's resources plus our own. This is the creed of the First Church of Partial Grace.

But, you see, partial grace will not cut it. It will not help; nor does it solve the problems. The humbling truth of the matter is that after the initial salvation by grace, from that moment on, we need a continual supply of strong grace from that time on. We must live daily before the Lord and each day must be "all of grace," "none of grace," or "half-and-half Christianity."

The "none of grace" style is dry and legalistic. This life of drudgery is effort after effort, and labor after labor with little or no joy. If persons only report grace as all-pervasive once in life or seldom, it may be that they've merely experienced a religious accident that is more serendipitous than other experiences. Grace is not an occasional, much less once-in-a-lifetime, occurrence; it happens all the time for the Christian. We live by grace, we eat by grace, we work by grace, we breathe by grace, we parent by grace, we live and die by grace. We will live in the week to come by grace.

Pity the person who thinks that he is saved by grace, only to walk the rest of the way by himself. God is not a quarterback who hands the ball off to us who are running backs, and then says, "Go the rest of the way yourself."

Neither does the hybrid approach work. "Half-and-half Christianity" will work no more than half-and-half salvation. It is not the case that we save ourselves half-way, and then God does the rest. On the contrary, the whole work of salvation is attributable to God.

Charles Spurgeon wrote a classic that Christians should read, *All of Grace*. If you're not familiar with Spurgeon, this morning I want to share a little of his life with you and a few snippets from one of his sermons that typifies the expansiveness of grace.

Charles Haddon Spurgeon (1834-1892) was a Baptist preacher, born in Kelvedon, Essex, of Dutch and Dissenting ancestry. His father and grandfather were Independent pastors. Early in 1850 he was converted in Artillery-street Primitive Methodist Chapel, Colchester, Essex, into which he came because of snowy weather. After baptism he became pastor of Waterbeach Baptist Chapel in 1851. As a 20-year old, in 1854 he was called to New Park Street Baptist Chapel, Southwark, London, which was soon filled to overflowing, necessitating the building of the Metropolitan Tabernacle in 1859.

In 1856 he began the "Pastor's College" for training men "evidently called to preach the Gospel," which continues today as "Spurgeon's College." For fifteen years he bore the whole cost, after which the Tabernacle shared the burden. In 1869 he established an orphanage at Stockwell, known now as "Spurgeon's Homes." He founded and supported several other charitable and religious organizations.

He preached at the Tabernacle for the last time on 7 June 1891 and died the following January at Mentone, France. During his 38-year London ministry he had built up a congregation of 6,000 and added 14,692 members to the church.

Spurgeon was an evangelical Calvinist. He read widely and especially loved the seventeenth century Puritans. A diverse author, he wrote biblical expositions, lectures to students, hymns, and the homely philosophy of "John Ploughman," among other works. Preeminently he was a preacher. His clear voice, his mastery of the English language, and his keen sense of humor, allied to a sure grasp of Scripture and a deep love for Christ, produced some of the noblest preaching of any age. His sermons have been printed and distributed throughout the world. Two popular works still widely used today are *Treasury of David* and *Morning and Evening*, the latter a compilation of devotional readings. [Source: *NIDCC*, 928]

In this chapter, I want you to focus with me on how God uses grace, in the beginning, middle, and end, in his people. We cannot live without grace, before we know Christ or afterwards.

1. First, look with me at The Beginning = Salvation by Grace.[46] To do so, focus with me on the well-known verse (Ephesians 2:8):

---

[46] Quotes in this chapters are taken from Spurgeon's Sermon (No. 3479);

"For by grace you are saved through faith; and that not of yourselves: it is the gift of God."—

Let me break this down into several parts. First, Spurgeon notes that:

I. There Is Present Salvation.

The apostle says, "You are saved." Not "you shall be," or "you may be"; but "you are saved." Neither does he say, "You are partly saved," nor "on the way to being saved," nor "hopeful of salvation"; but "by grace you are saved." Let us be as clear on this point as he was, and let us never rest till we know that we are saved. At this moment we are either saved or unsaved. That is clear. To which class do you belong? I hope that, by the witness of the Holy Ghost, you may be so assured of your safety as to sing, "The Lord is my strength and my song; he is my salvation." Salvation is a present reality. Let me pass on to note the next point.

II. A Present Salvation Must Be Through Grace.

If we can say of any man, or of any set of people, "You are saved," we shall have to preface it with the words "by grace." There is no other present salvation except that which begins and ends with grace. As far as I know, I do not think that anyone in the wide world pretends to preach or to possess a present salvation, except those who believe salvation to be all of grace. . . . Some few Catholics may hope to enter heaven when they die, but most of them have the miserable prospect of purgatory before their eyes. We see constant requests for prayers for departed souls, and this would not be if those souls were saved, and glorified with their Savior.

Among those who dwell around us, we find many who are [altogether] total strangers to the doctrine of grace, and these never dream of present salvation. Possibly they trust that they may be saved when they die; they half hope that, after years of watchful holiness, they may, perhaps, be saved at last; but, to be saved now,

---

Thursday, October 7th, 1915.

and to know that they are saved, is quite beyond them, and they think it presumption.

There can be no present salvation unless it be upon this footing—"By grace are you saved." It is a very striking [singular] thing that no one has risen up to preach a present salvation by works. I suppose it would be too absurd. The works being unfinished, the salvation would be incomplete; or, the salvation being complete, the main motive of the legalist would be gone.

Salvation must be *by grace*. If man is lost by sin, how can he be saved except through the grace of God? If he has sinned, he is condemned; and how can he, of himself, reverse that condemnation? Suppose that he should keep the law all the rest of his life, he will then only have done what he was always bound to have done, and he will still be an unprofitable servant. What is to become of the past? How can old sins be blotted out? How can the old ruin be retrieved? According to Scripture, and according to common sense, salvation can only be through the free favor of God.

Salvation in the present tense must be by the *free favor of God*. People may contend for salvation by works, but you will not hear anyone support his own argument by saying, "I am myself saved by what I have done." Pride could hardly [contain] itself with such extravagant boasting. No, if we are saved, it must be by the free favor of God. No one professes to be an example of the opposite view.

Salvation *to be complete must be by free favor*. The saints, when they come to die, never conclude their lives by hoping in their good works. Those who have lived the most holy and useful lives invariably look to free grace in their final moments. I never stood by the bedside of a godly man who reposed any confidence whatever in his own prayers, or repentance, or religiousness. I have heard eminently holy men quoting in death the words, "Christ Jesus came into the world to save sinners." In fact, the nearer men come to heaven, and the more prepared they are for it, the more simply is their trust in the merit of the Lord Jesus, and the more intensely they abhor all trust in themselves. If this is the case in our last moments, when the conflict is almost over, we ought to feel it more so while we are in the thick of the fight. If a man is completely saved in this present time of warfare, how can it be except by grace? While he has to mourn over sin that dwells in him, while he has to confess innumerable shortcomings and transgressions, while sin is mixed with all he does, how can he believe that he is completely saved except it be by the free favor of God?

Paul speaks of this salvation as belonging to the Ephesians, "By grace are you saved." The Ephesians had been given to curious arts and works of divination. They had thus made a covenant with the powers of darkness. Now if such as these were saved, it must be by grace alone. So is it with us also: our original condition and character render it certain that, if saved at all, we must owe it to the free favor of God.

III. Present Salvation by Grace Must Be Through Faith.

A present salvation must be through grace, and salvation by grace must be through faith. You cannot get a hold of salvation by grace by any other means than by faith. This live coal from off the altar needs the golden tongs of faith with which to carry it.

Rule out the following: Salvation is *not by works.*

It might have been possible, if God had so willed it, that salvation might have been through works, and yet by grace; for if Adam had perfectly obeyed the law of God, still he would only have done what he was bound to do; and so, if God should have rewarded him, the reward itself must have been according to grace, since the Creator owes nothing to the creature. This would have been a very difficult system to work, while the object of it was perfect; but in our case it would not work at all. Salvation in our case means deliverance from guilt and ruin, and this could not have been laid hold of by a measure of good works, since we are not in a condition to perform any.

Suppose I preached that sinners must do certain works, and then you would be saved; and suppose that you could perform them; such a salvation would not then have been seen to be altogether of grace; it would have soon appeared to be of debt. [In that case], it would have come to you in some measure as the reward of work done, and its whole [complexion] would have been changed. Salvation by grace can only be gripped by the hand of faith: the attempt to lay hold upon it by the doing of certain acts of law would cause the grace to evaporate. "Therefore, it is of faith that it might be by grace." "If by grace, then it is no more of works: otherwise grace is no more grace. But if it be of works, then it is no more grace: otherwise work is no more work."

Some try to lay hold upon salvation by grace through the *use of ceremonies;* but it will not do. You may have been baptized, confirmed, and . . . join the church, or sit at the Lord's table: does this bring you salvation? I ask, "As wonderful as these are, does this bring salvation?

Again, salvation by grace is not *through your feelings*. The hand of faith [not feeling] is constructed for the grasping of a present salvation by grace. If you say, "I must feel that I am saved. I must feel so much sorrow and so much joy or else I will not admit that I am saved," you will find that this method will not answer. As much as you might hope to see with your ear, or taste with your eye, or hear with your nose, as to believe by feeling: it is the wrong organ. After you have believed, you can enjoy salvation by feeling its heavenly influences; but to dream of getting a grasp of it by your own feelings is as foolish as to attempt to bear away the sunlight in the palm of your hand. There is an essential absurdity in the whole affair.

Moreover, the evidence yielded by feeling is singularly fickle. When your feelings are peaceful and delightful, they are soon broken in upon, and become restless and melancholy. The most fickle of elements, the most feeble of creatures, the most contemptible circumstances, may sink or raise your spirits: experienced men come to think less and less of their present emotions as they reflect upon the little reliance which can be safely placed upon them. Faith receives the statement of God concerning his way of gracious pardon, and thus it brings salvation to the man believing; but feeling, warming under passionate appeals, yielding itself deliriously to a hope which it dares not examine, whirling round and round in a sort of dervish dance of excitement which has become necessary for its own sustaining, is all on a stir, like the troubled sea which cannot rest. From its boilings and ragings, feeling may drop to lukewarmness, despondency, despair and all the kindred evils. Feelings cannot be trusted in reference to the eternal verities of God. We now go a step further:—

IV. Salvation by Grace, Through Faith, Is Not of Ourselves.
The salvation and the faith and the whole gracious work together are not of ourselves.

First, they are *not of our former deservings*: they are not the reward of former good endeavours. No unregenerate person has lived so well that God is bound to give him further grace, and to bestow on him eternal life; else it were no longer of grace, but of debt. Salvation is given to us, not earned by us. Our first life is always a wandering away from God, and our new life of return to God is always a work of undeserved mercy, wrought upon those who greatly need, but never deserve it.

It is not of ourselves, in the further sense, that it is *not out of our original excellence. Salvation comes from above; it is never evolved from within.* Can eternal life be evolved from the bare ribs of death? Some dare to tell us that faith in Christ, and the new birth, are only the development of good things that lay hidden in us by nature; but in this, like their father, they speak of their own. You may take the unregenerate man, and educate him to the highest; but he remains, and must forever remain, dead in sin, unless a higher power shall come in and save him from himself. Grace brings into the heart an entirely foreign element. It does not improve and perpetuate; it kills and makes alive. There is no continuity between the state of nature and the state of grace: the one is darkness and the other is light; the one is death and the other is life.

Salvation by grace, through faith is not of ourselves in the sense of being the result of our own power. We are bound to view salvation as being as surely a divine act as creation, or providence, or resurrection. At every point of the process of salvation this word is appropriate—"not of yourselves." From the first desire after it to the full reception of it by faith, it is evermore of the Lord alone, and not of ourselves. The man believes, but that belief is only one result among many of the implantation of divine life within the man's soul by God himself.

Even the very will thus to be saved by grace is not of ourselves, but it is the gift of God. But man ... prefers anything to faith in his redeemer. Unless the Spirit of God convinces the judgment, and constrains the will, man has no heart to believe in Jesus unto eternal life. *I ask any saved man to look back upon his own conversion and explain how it came about.* You turned to Christ, and believed in his name: But what **caused** you thus to turn? What sacred force was that which turned you from sin to righteousness? Do you attribute this singular renewal to the existence of a something better in you than has been yet discovered in your unconverted neighbor? No, you confess that you might have been what he now is if it had not been that there was a potent something which touched the spring of your will, enlightened your understanding, and guided you to the foot of the cross.

Gratefully we confess the fact; it must be so. Salvation by grace, through faith, is not of ourselves, and none of us would dream of taking any honor to ourselves from our conversion, or from any gracious effect which has flowed from the first divine cause.

V. "By Grace Are Ye Saved Through Faith; and That Not of Yourselves: It Is the Gift of God."

Salvation may be called . . . God's gift. Multiply your phrases, and expand your expositions; but salvation truly traced to its well-head is all contained in the gift unspeakable, the free, unmeasured present of love. Salvation is the gift of God, in opposition to a wage. When a man pays another his wage, he does what is right; and no one dreams of lauding him for it. But we praise God for salvation because it is not the payment of debt, but the gift of grace. No man enters eternal life on earth, or in heaven, as his due:

it is the gift of God. We say, "nothing is freer than a gift." Salvation is so purely, so absolutely a gift of God, that nothing can be more free.

God gives it because he chooses to give it, according to that grand text which has made many a man bite his lip in wrath, "I will have mercy on whom I will have mercy, I will have compassion on whom I will have compassion."

You are all guilty and condemned, and the great King pardons whom he wills from among you. This is his royal prerogative. He saves in infinite sovereignty of grace.

Salvation is the gift of God: that is to say completely so, in opposition to the notion of growth. Salvation is not a natural production from within: it is brought from a foreign zone, and planted within the heart by heavenly hands. If you will have it, there it is, complete and in its entirety a gift from God. Will you have it as a perfect gift? "Some answer: No; I will produce it in my own workshop." But you cannot forge a work so rare and costly, upon which even Jesus spent his life's blood. Here is a garment without seam, woven from the top throughout. It will cover you and make you glorious. Will you have it? "No; I will sit at the loom, and I will weave a [garment] of my own!" That is the answer of a proud fool. That is spinning cobwebs, weaving a dream. Rather, take what Christ upon the cross declared to be finished.

It is the gift of God: that is, it is eternally secure in opposition to the gifts of men, which soon pass away. "Not as the world gives, give I unto you," says our Lord Jesus. If my Lord Jesus gives you salvation at this moment, you have it, and you have it forever. He will never take it back again; and if he does not take it from you, who can? If he saves you now through faith, you are saved—so saved that you shall never perish, neither shall any pluck you out of his hand.

Over these many years, this is the sum of my faith. Within the circle of these words my theology is contained, so far as it refers to the salvation of men. I rejoice also to remember that those of my family who were ministers of Christ before me preached this doctrine, and none other. My father, who is still able to bear his personal testimony for his Lord, knows no other doctrine, neither did his father before him.

I remember a somewhat singular circumstance, recorded in my memory that connects this text to my grandfather. Years ago, I was to preach in a certain country town in the Eastern Counties. . . . Punctuality is one of those little virtues which may prevent great sins. But we have no control over railway delays, and break-downs; and so I reached the appointed place considerably behind the time. Like sensible people, they had begun their worship, and had proceeded as far as the sermon. As I neared the chapel, I saw someone in the pulpit preaching, and it was my dear, venerable grandfather! He saw me as I came in at the front door and made my way up the aisle, and at once he said, "Here comes my grandson! He may preach the gospel better than I can, but he cannot preach a better gospel; can you, Charles?" As I made my way through the throng, I answered, "You can preach better than I can. Pray go on." But he would not agree to that. I must take the sermon, and so I did, going on with the subject there and then, just where he left off. "There," said he, "I was preaching of 'For by grace are ye saved.' I have been setting forth the source and fountain-head of salvation; and I am now showing them the channel of it, through faith. Now you take it up, and go on." I am so much at home with these glorious truths that I could not feel any difficulty in taking from my grandfather the thread of his discourse, and joining my thread to it, so as to continue without a break.

Our agreement in the things of God made it easy for us to be joint-preachers of the same discourse. I went on with "through faith," and then I proceeded to the next point, "and that not of yourselves." Upon this I was explaining the weakness and inability of human nature, and the certainty that salvation could not be of ourselves, when I had my coat-tail pulled, and my well-beloved grandsire took his turn again. "When I spoke of our depraved human nature," the good old man said, "I know most about that, dear friends"; and so . . . for the next five minutes set forth a solemn and humbling description of our lost estate, the depravity of our nature, and the spiritual death under which we were found. When he had said his say in a very gracious manner, his grandson was allowed to go on again, to the dear old man's great delight; for now and then he would say, in a gentle tone, "Good! Good!" Once he said, "Tell them that again, Charles," and, of course, I did tell them that again. It was a happy exercise to me to take my share in bearing witness to truths of such vital importance, which are so deeply impressed upon my heart. While announcing this text I seem to hear that dear voice, which has been so long lost to earth, saying to me, "TELL THEM THAT AGAIN." I am not contradicting the testimony of forefathers who are now with God. If my grandfather could return to earth, he would find me where he left me, steadfast in the faith, and true to that form of doctrine which was once delivered to the saints. Will you remain in "All of Grace?"

B. But just as grace began, it also continues to be the principle of Christian living long after salvation. Many church-goers have not grasped this. It is not too much to say that: Grace continues to animate the believer his whole life, just as in the beginning of his spiritual walk. Look with me at the description of Christians as:

Grace-Epistles in 2 Corinthians 2:14-3:18

God calls us written letters, "a letter from Christ . . . written not with ink but with the Spirit of the living God, not on tablets of stone but on tablets of human hearts." (2 Cor. 3:3)

How can we, sinful as we are, be epistles to the world from God? Wouldn't that hopelessly taint the message? The only answer is that we become such by grace. God takes care of our deficiencies, removes our guilt, and reconstructs us for his own glory.

Verse 5 makes it plain that the secret of this grace is not because of talents or abilities we may have: "Not that we are competent to claim anything for ourselves, but our competence comes from God."

Are you at a place in your life where you can admit that even your competence, your very abilities are attributable to God's grace? We are competent to serve him—not because we have been well trained, not because we've had good mentors, and certainly not because we have superb abilities. Rather, it is by grace that we live and serve God. So we not only COME to Christ by grace; we also CONTINUE in Christ by grace.

As the Christian matures, there is more grace and more glory of Christ. It is not the case that we peak at salvation and then decline in grace from then on. Rather, it is all of grace. Every day, every moment, every success, and every difficulty must be and can only be met with the grace of Christ. That is what transforms us, and that is what animates us.

When was the last time you spent some time with a dying saint? Or a person with an incurable illness? And don't you find that believer rise to those occasions in unbelievable ways? It is because of present grace. These people are trophies of grace. It is all of grace.

Religious schemes, even righteous techniques and spiritual disciplines, will not transform us. It takes something larger than ourselves to do that. That "something" is God's grace. His glory transforms us; his grace is ever-increasing.

That's why Spurgeon and others can talk of "all of grace." It is.

Are you ready to admit that, and live by that standard? Or do you still occasionally (or normally) hold out for human standards? Do you still want God to consider you partially in terms of what Christ has done for you, and then partially in terms of what you can do for yourselves? That will not lead to grace or glory. It may produce self-righteousness or self-confidence, but it will not produce living epistles.

We NEED to be more dependent on God. Everyday, we need to come back to his grace and dwell on it more.

Epilogue:

Let me briefly mention another important part of Spurgeon's life and continuing testimony. He held the strongest of views about

Grace. But that reliance on grace did not turn him into a free-thinker, nor a liberal. I hate to say it, but at times, some people frighten me a little. When they flirt with or discover grace for the first time, often there is an accompanying lawlessness that sometimes leads to an abandonment of Christian morality and the difficult areas of biblical faith. Neither Spurgeon nor the Apostle Paul believed that grace should lead to lawlessness.

Spurgeon witnessed one of the earliest forms of liberalism which has been many times repeated here in our countries. It was called the "Downgrade controversy." This name signified the all-too-ready willingness of church leaders to downgrade doctrines or practices that were out of favor. This 'dumbing down' of evangelical Christianity was a retreat in the face of liberalism. Spurgeon resisted it. When other leaders thought that the Trinity was too ancient, the doctrine of Hell too scary, the call of Christ too demanding for a Victorian England, and when the exclusivism of the biblical faith countered the liberalism of the modern church, Spurgeon stood against the breach and opposed the downgrading of Christianity. This experience only reinforced his ardent Calvinism, which many a Baptist today will ignore or even try to explain away.

Chapter 11

The Sovereignty of God (A. W. Pink): Good News or Bad News?

Romans 8:28-30

"One man's heaven is another man's hell."

"The cup is half-empty or half-full, depending on how you look at it."

Predestination, is it Good news or bad news?

Many people think that predestination is either bad news or an unbiblical teaching. I know no other way to introduce this controversial topic to you, other than just to spell it out, like the scriptures have it. Let me tell you a little-known secret, too: "Most Presbyterians do not know what the Bible teaches on this subject. They only go on tradition." Don't make the mistake of assuming that just because Presbyterians have been known for pre-destination for centuries, that today all are aware of that.

Some churches may be a little different. Some of you may have studied this, and grappled with it. Some have even changed their mind. I find, by the way, that when persons have minds that are even a little open, they frequently come to adopt this biblical teaching. However, I don't find many people, who once they believe in this, move away from it. Interestingly, this article of faith has real staying power.

Indulge me in a short apology (not "I'm sorry" but rationale for why), since this is such an important area. I have never preached on this subject in my first years in a pastorate, lest listeners think I'm crazy. In our most recent church, I did not preach on this topic until my 9th year at that church, and even though these chapters are among my personal favorites, I've not preached from these rich sections of the Bible, primarily in an attempt to avoid ramming predestination down throats too fast. Perhaps I've been remiss. We who believe fervently in something, and know the opposite, do have to be careful that our zeal does not multiply stumbling blocks.

So I've tried to be careful. However, I'm not going to really do what I threatened privately (to Ann, my wife) that I would do. Some time back, in a church where I served, I heard people say that a Pastor had no business ever publicly expounding these doctrines because they were too controversial. You've heard that kind of comment before. And indeed it would be difficult to carry out a ministry, if one had to continually tip-toe through the mine-fields of controversy, always peeping this way or that, to make sure he wasn't ruffling anyone's feathers. To do that, you would almost have to cut whole pages out of the Bible, as Thomas Jefferson did.

I'm not going to do like I threatened, and totally skip Rom. 8-9 (although the effect would be dramatic). God's Word is too precious, too rich, and too full, for us to apply the Jeffersonian scissors to those passages of scripture that we don't particularly agree with, especially if the cause of disagreement is with our natural nature. If I were to avoid controversy, I'd have to skip the following from Romans chapter 8:

v. 28
v. 29
v. 30
(keep 31-32)
v. 33 - "elect" - all of which is the foundation of the last part of Rom. 8

All of Romans 9 would have to be skipped. We'd have a shredded Bible. If we avoid this topic, we would necessarily avoid some of the most comforting, best parts of scripture. Do you think God would have put this in the Bible, if he didn't want us to dwell and expound it? I think not.

My friend Steve Lawson, was once warned by the head deacon not to preach on Romans 8, lest it disturb people. The faithful pastor inquired why and, faithful to his calling, went ahead, although he was asked to leave a prestigious pulpit. But it was more important to him to be faithful to God's Word than to gain the approval of men. I admire his courage and his fidelity. We need more like that.

At the outset we have to decide before we can ever accept God's teaching on this specific, if we will accept his teaching at all. Predestination is a matter of biblical faithfulness. If we reject it, we reject large sections of God's Word, an editorial feat which he has not called us to perform.

So why is this topic so hard?

I am certainly aware that in our own time and in our community, those who hold to this ancient truth are in the minority. So, if the standard is majority rule, like in many other things, then we who stick to scripture lose the vote and should become Mormons or Muslim. Unfortunately, in modern times, we lost the debate so long ago, that we haven't been able to recapture it. That is for a future day, but I believe God has you and me here today to start today. It is a tragic sadness that presbyterians of all people lost the insight and comfort of this amazing part of our salvation.

You know, one of the things I find most amazing about Christians is how selective we are. We keep wanting to pick and choose our way to heaven. We want some things that God has, but don't want to accept others. Why, we even memorize partial verses. That always amazes me. Let me test you. I want to demonstrate to you how selective, and dangerously selective, we are in scripture memory. Close your Bibles.

Complete these sentences below:

A "Judge not, lest . . ."

Now recite for me, the next line..... (this is normally memorized out of context)

B "For it is by grace that you have been saved through faith . . ." (Eph. 2:8-9)
Now tell me the next part?

C Now fill this in: "We know that in all things God works . . ."
What follows?

You see, this very verse where we begin today, is a perfect example of selective memorization. Many people have clung to this script in bad times. When times are bad, we recite, "in all things God works for the good of those who love him." Then we reason out a short little chain, "I love him; therefore, all things will work out OK." That brings tremendous comfort. I've clung to that many a time and will in the future.

But did you notice, if you open back your bibles, or if you memorized correctly, that the verse does not end where its most common memorization ends. It goes on and tells us how this verse belongs to those who have *been called*. It tells us a lot more, too.

Let's see what God's word really says. Would you listen to God's Word this morning? See if it really says these things.

God's categorical promise— v. 28a

Good things stand on their own merit. This verse is like a Rembrandt. The reason that a truly great piece of art stands the test of time is because it is truly great. That is why this verse has nourished so many. And it will continue to do so. It gives us God's categorical promise, a kind of promise that nothing else in the world can give. Further, it is given to us, by the God who can bring all his promises about.

When believers put this verse to the test, they see how strong it is. This is part of why I want to tell you the pre-destination is not bad news, but good news.

First it is stated that God works in all things. This verse does not assert that God works in a few areas, or leaves all the blanks to be filled in by us. Neither does it teach that God passively resigns some of his sovereignty, to let others work all things out.

Instead, in the clear language of scripture, God works in all things - not just some. Does that mean, that he works in:

Cancer ?
Loss of job?
disappointment?
Election of leaders?
national destinies?

Yes, it says "all things," and unless we pervert the language, we cannot escape the truth that God is really as great and all-working, as this says. That's why some people want to clip this chapter out of their Bible. Because, if God is doing these things, then we have no room left for complaining, or grumbling, or self-righteous assertion of our wills over his.

For the Christian, however, this is not bad news. It is only so for the rebellious, self-willed person, trying to create their only small sovereignty. For the Christian, it is great news to know that God is working, and working so effectively and wonderfully. God works in all things, as superbly as he works salvation. We rejoice that he is working. The alternative is the loitering God, the God who is in retirement, resting, never interfering, an enfeebled impotent God, who must let the creatures call all the shots. This theological perversion writ-large is contrary to this verse.

God has given his people a categorical promise, one that lives and communities can indeed be built upon. We can plan for the future, and move ahead in godly confidence with this truth residing within us.

It's wonderful to know that our success, or the effect of this promise, is not dependent on circumstances. Look over this verse. I don't see a disclaimer anywhere. I don't see that there is a caveat stating that under some conditions, this will not come about. It says in all things God works for the good of those . . . Even if doesn't seem like it, it still is.

I want you to know before we go any further, that God is working on the behalf of his people, day in and day out, behind the scenes . . . and for their good. He has a goal in mind, and he is busily bringing about good for his people. Isn't that good news? That he goes before you and prepares a way, and provides good for you? That is part of what predestination is.

However, this is limited to the recipients to whom it properly belongs. This promise, unfortunately, does not belong to everyone. The verse, while categorical, is not unconditional. It is presented as a promise for a groups described by two terms. It is normally, only the first which is memorized. But there are two.

The first description is that this is true for those who "love him." To love the Lord is a simple act. It need not have lengthy explanation. We all know what love is. But do we love God? Or are we off loving ourselves? For all who love God, this verse is assuredly true.

Nevertheless, there is another description, which is frequently overlooked. And it takes us behind a veil. This categorical promise is true for those who love God, who are also the ones "who have been called according to his purpose"

This gives us a:

Prelude to the promise, 28b

In terms of order, God's purpose comes first. Long before we love him, or respond to him, he must call us, if we are to ever love.

In fact, if you look ahead, you'll see that this last part of v. 28, the oft-ignored part, is what takes us right into the subject of pre-destination. Not only has God called his people, but this very same group is spoken about as: God's work before we even know.

According to scripture, God works together all things for those who love him and have been called *according to his purpose*. The word for "purpose" refers to his eternal decree or plan. So, the plan/decree comes first. Then God calls us, and in the end we love him.

The very next verse states the same truth all over again, just in slightly different words. "Those" (i. e., same as above) God foreknew he also predestined. Stop briefly to understand the meaning of these two words. *What would you say, if I told you that these 2 words were so difficult that no ordinary person could understand them?* If you wouldn't believe that, I'm glad. Because it's not true. Actually these words are so simple that a five-year old can understand.

One word (foreknow) means to "know ahead of time," and whenever God knows something ahead of time, it is because he has already mapped it out.

The other word pre-destine, means to "plan out an end ahead of time". . . pre-destiny. What's hard about that? Actually nothing. In fact sometimes, young people can see through these things and comprehend better than adults.

I found that a youth group of 7th-9th graders forced me to accept the Bible on this point once. Below is my story of how a good Methodist like me came to embrace pre-destination. Believe me, I was sort of like the Fonz on *Happy Days* trying to apologize. He just couldn't speak the words "I was wrong." I, too, could hardly mention this word. Let alone, say I heartily believed it.

I was raised in a Methodist home, and we believed in free will. After I became a Christian, I became more and more convinced that the Bible was the only possible guide for life that was reliable and true. So I committed myself to the scriptures, and wanted to follow them wherever they led. I attended a leading seminary with high emphasis on scripture. I studied under convinced Calvinists for four years and still upon graduation did not fully embrace these teachings. I could not honestly take the officer vows for the denomination where I now serve. So I went into a more liberal church where anything was allowed.

While working with young people in a small town in north Georgia, I led many bible studies, and challenged the kids to follow the Bible. I taught them that "the Bible means what it says, and says what it means." Once, I was leading a bible study with these young Christians—fresh converts—and we got to this same passage. An 8th grader asked me what predestination meant. And I answered, "Oh don't worry about it, it doesn't really mean what it looks like it says." My well-trained youth troops jumped on me, and I realized I had committed the very fallacy I had so often warned them against. I had to adjourn immediately, go home, and study.

I eventually reached the conclusion that predestination really did mean what it said, and that God does have a plan, that he has decreed before any sprig was on this earth, and that it's coming about is as certain as God. Moreover, THAT'S GOOD. Not bad.

Amazingly frequent in scripture

Predestination and election are taught all throughout scripture. I haven't possibly the time to refer to each passage. But consider a few:

Eph. 1

2 Thess.

Mt.

Neither is this just a NT teaching.

Gen. 45:7-8 and 50:20

Now you have to ask, if this is so biblical and repeated so often, just *why some don't like it. Three main reasons to reject:*

1. Folks either misunderstand, thinking it will be a disincentive to:
      prayer
      missions
      evangelism/missions
      giving

service

It is certainly not. The Pre-destination of God never annuls a commandment of God.

2. Folks don't like the fact, that Someone else makes our decisions.
Ahh! Many people find that they just don't like the idea of somebody being their boss, or pulling the strings that they cannot pull.

3. This might mean that one of their relatives of friends will not be in heaven.
However, it is hardly more comforting to think our loved ones are in hell because of their own free choices. The temperatures, best I can tell, are no lower if related to free choice.

Predestination is part of the "Order of salvation"
Theologians have spoken of this as the "order of salvation," and it is indeed a biblical concept, which is represented here. Although we may not be fully conscious of each individual step, it is important to see how the scripture does teach such a pattern or order. If we can sense this big picture, then the parts fit together a little better.
Several scriptures teach this. John 1:12 is a common memory verse for many new Christians. There is an order of salvation, and verse 13 speaks of those who become God's children. Yet they do not become that way because of natural birth, nor of some decision or will of a human father. God's children are "born of God." Rebirth is more fundamental, and must come first, before we "Receive-and-Believe." In fact, we will neither receive nor believe, until we are first born again. That's what scripture and confession teach.
John 3, the well-known episode with Nicodemus, contains a definite order. Jesus himself says that things must follow a certain order if a person hopes to see the Kingdom of God. That will not come, unless first there is a rebirth process. The Lord of our salvation announced the steps and pre-requisites: "No one can see

the Kingdom of God unless he is born again (Jn. 3:3) . . . No one can enter the Kingdom of God unless he is born of water and the Spirit (Jn. 3:5). Thus being born again precedes any spiritual insight or inheritance of eternal life.

Romans 10 also teaches this. Verse 13 of that chapter promises that anyone "who calls on the name of the Lord will be saved." However, as that section of scripture continues, it makes it clear that this act of confession only occurs following other basic aspects related to our salvation. As that passage works its way backwards in chronology, it tells us that no one makes that confession without internal belief (10:14), and that such belief will not be there unless the person "hears" the call. And people will not hear the call, without the preaching of God's Word, and the preachers of God's Word must be commissioned (10:15) to go and bear the good news. The chain in this passage is that the Church sends preachers, who preach the Word so that people can hear the message. After hearing the message, those who are God's people will believe, and then will confess the Lord. And assuredly, all who call on the Lord will be saved.

Perhaps one of the clearest places where this is explained is Romans 8:30-32. This passage goes on to show that those who have been called according to God's purpose are also then the objects of his predestination, his calling, his justifying, and his glorifying (all in 8:30). Hence God, beginning with his purpose (decree) predestines, calls, justifies and keeps; so that all who are somewhere in the midst of that process can certainly know that all things will work together for good. This order of salvation gives meaning to the assurance to which so many of us cling in that wonderful memory verse.

Also to see the interconnectedness of Christian experience, one could study Romans 5:3-5 and 2 Peter 1:5-9. In both of those, growth in grace, or the maturation of Christian virtues are heaped upon one another as God does his work in our lives. Apparent in scripture is a basic pattern, in which God takes us from death to life, from unbelief to trust, and this "so great salvation" (Heb. 2:3) is a package deal, which flowers into many different aspects, and into eternity.

Ephesians 2:1-10 is another fine passage, which incorporates nearly all of the individual steps of salvation as laid out. The first 3 verses of this passage indicate that before any person comes to Christ, that person is "dead in transgressions and sins" (2:1), a follower of the "ruler of the kingdom of the air, the spirit who is now at work in those who are disobedient" (2:2), intent on "gratifying the cravings of our sinful nature" (2:3), and "by nature, objects of wrath" (2:3). This was our pre-Christian state, and we could not have the faith of Eph. 2:8-9, without a dramatic interruption by God.

So the order is that into this sin-dominated life comes God's rich mercy (Eph. 2:4). Then, while we were still dead (cf. also Rom. 5:6-10), prior to our seeing the kingdom of God (Jn. 3:3, 5), God who is rich in mercy "made us alive with Christ even when we were dead in transgressions- it is by grace you have been saved" (2:5). As to order, God's work comes before our conscious faith. We are reborn, or "made alive with Christ"; then we can respond in faith, following rebirth. In addition, after this rebirth, the outworking of this salvation continues into the "coming ages" so that Christians can live lives that "show the incomparable riches of his grace" (Eph. 2:7).

Then verses 8-10 inform us that grace is foundational, i. e., that this grace which comes from God generates even our faith "-and this [is] not from yourselves, it is the gift of God" (2:8). These verses are clear that the work of salvation is in no way from ourselves, nor from our own works (2:9). The entire work is begun and affected by the mighty grace of God. This work does not end only in our salvation; it extends to our living out a Christian life as the "workmanship of God," who have been created in Christ Jesus to do good works "which God prepared in advance for us to do" (Eph. 2:10). Hence we can see the order of salvation and the scope of God's work in these verses.

This Order in v. 30 is true of all Christians. It is not a special privilege given only to some, or one class of Christians.

Note also: All are in passive voice (God does these, not we ourselves)

Finally, note the payoff, or what affect this has on us in v. 31: "If God is for us, who can be against us? The answer is No One. Come back next time to learn more of this. But for now, I hope you've begun to see why pre-destination is such good news. It is part of, and at the heart of, the greatest news. God gave us this, and I hope you won't cheat yourself by twisting this into bad news.

Several co-workers in Tennessee decided to have a bible study together. They were memorizing and discussing scripture together on their lunch hour. There was one Presbyterian and three Baptists (typical odds in the south). And one of the Baptists refused to memorize a verse? What, you say, are the Baptists giving up the Bible? Not at all. Of many they hold to it most strictly. He refused to memorize this verse because it had overtones of pre-destination.

Ah," you say, "so the Presbyterian was being obnoxious, trying to sneak in his partisan bias." That's why the Baptist wouldn't touch this verse. What was the verse? It was Ephesians 2:8, not exactly the private property of presbyterians.

Why didn't this fellow want to consider this verse? Because he knew where the Presbyterian thought it led. And he didn't want to follow that rich verse, even if from the Bible, wherever it led. I wonder, are you a person like that? At times you see a verse, and you're smart enough to know where it leads. You just don't want to go there.

I want to call on you this morning to say "yes" to God. To say yes, I'll follow your Word wherever it leads, even if into uncharted territory for me and my family. You'll find a lot of excellent company. Don't tell God no.

And this topic brings great comfort, based on this:

1. If Christ predestines and justifies, who can condemn?
2. If Christ predestines and justifies, nothing can separate

This is why believers love this so much! This is profoundly good news.

Chapter 12

The Cost of Discipleship (Bonhoeffer)

Luke 9:57-61; Luke 14:25-33; 2 Timothy 2:2

On January 30, 1933, Adolf Hitler became chancellor of Germany. Within three months he had managed to destroy democracy in Germany and institute himself as the nation's dictator. On April 7 of the same year, Hitler pushed through the "Law for the Restoration of the Civil Service," the first major anti-Jewish statute of the new era. One provision of this law, the so-called Aryan Clause, forced all persons defined as Jewish out of the civil service, including the universities and the churches.

Later that month, Dietrich Bonhoeffer addressed a discussion group of German pastors. His talk, "The Church and the Jewish Question," is widely recognized as the earliest and best response of any church leader to these early expressions of Nazi anti-Semitism. He argued that the church has the obligation to challenge the state when it misuses its power; to aid anyone, including Jews, when they are victimized by the state; and ultimately, to "jam a spoke in the wheel" of the state if it continues to crush people. Some pastors left indignantly during his talk, thinking it too "political," too "radical," and too friendly to the Jews.

Bonhoeffer's most intense involvement in the German "Church Struggle" occurred between April and October 1933 (at which time he left Germany to take a pastorate in London). He was aghast at Hitler's nazification of the churches and at the massive cooperation the Fuhrer found within German Protestantism, especially its adoption in September 1933 of the Aryan Clause as official policy. This introduction of state-mandated racism into church life was, for Bonhoeffer, nothing less than heresy.

In 1934, a church meeting composed of 600 German ministers and theological professors actually adopted this resolution: "We are full of thanks to God that he, as Lord of history, has given us Adolf Hitler, our leader and savior from our difficult lot. We acknowledge that we, with body and soul, are bound and dedicated to the German state and to its Fuhrer. This bondage and duty contains for us, as evangelical Christians, its deepest and most holy significance in its obedience to the command of God."

Bonhoeffer resisted relentlessly and publicly, but he and his allies did not succeed in keeping control of the German Evangelical Church. In an attempt to preserve the integrity of German Protestantism, indeed, to keep alive authentic witness to Jesus Christ and fidelity to the Word of God, in May 1934 the Confessing Church came into being. Its famous *Barmen Declaration* denounced "the idolatrous acquiescence to Nazi church policies" within the officially sanctioned Protestant church. The Confessing Church would become the headquarters of the Protestant resistance in Germany.

If we fast-forward to the end of his life, early in the morning of April 9, 1945, German theologian and churchman Dietrich Bonhoeffer was executed in Flossenburg concentration camp for his part in a conspiracy to assassinate Adolf Hitler. Flossenburg's doctor testified to Bonhoeffer's last moments:

Pastor Bonhoeffer, before taking off his prison garb, [knelt] on the floor praying fervently to his God. I was most deeply moved by the way this lovable man prayed, so devout and so certain that God heard his prayer . . . At the place of execution he again said a short prayer and then

climbed to the steps of the gallows, brave and composed . . . I have
hardly ever seen a man die so entirely submissive to the will of God.[47]

This man counted the costs of following Christ, especially
when it meant opposing a corrupt and sinful political leader.

Dietrich Bonhoeffer . . . hanging from a gallows. It is a scene
by now deeply etched in Christian consciousness, a scene of
extraordinary significance both for Bonhoeffer's time and for ours.
One of the first books handed to many a new Christian in our day
is Dietrich Bonhoeffer's *The Cost of Discipleship*. It is a comment
on our day that many Christian leaders feel the need to stress that
so much. Evidently, many leaders believe that the proper emphasis
on costs is being ignored to some degree.

Mentoring is the new buzz-word in many Christian circles. The
best I can tell, the concepts of mentoring, apprenticeship, and
discipleship—all which reflect on-the-job training—are nearly the
same. And each of them—whatever phrase you want to use—was
taught best by Jesus.

So what is discipleship? To many, it is simply the
mathematical formula by which one could (theoretically) reach the
world for Christ in our generation. The first time I heard this
concept, it was from a Campus Crusade for Christ [now called
"Cru", dropping the overt reference to Christ!] worker, who
explained it to me roughly like this: If you were successfully to
evangelize 1,000 people per day—every one of whom came to
Christ, truly and remained with him—each day of your life, it
would take 100,000 years to reach all the people in the world. That
is expansion by ADDITION. However, discipleship employs
MULTIPLICATION, i. e., you can reach the world much faster if
you reach others and then train them to multiply. In contrast to the
method of addition above, if you disciple/train only 4 persons/year
(and do it right), and then next year, each of those 4 (plus yourself)
train 4 each; then the following year, each of those 25 can train 4;
then the next year, those 125 can train 4 each, etc., until the entire

---

[47] Source: R. C. Sproul, *Study Guide on Providence* (Orlando: Ligonier
Ministries, 1990), 63.

world could be reached in a generation. Discipleship—the training of others to train others—is a concept that assists in the worldwide spread of the gospel. Moreover, not only does discipleship aid in **quantity**, but the **quality** of disciples would be much higher if trained intensely for a year in a small group, rather than one of 365,000 converted in a crusade with no follow-up.

One verse that is used to illustrate this is 2 Timothy 2:2: "And the things you have heard me say in the presence of many witnesses entrust to reliable men who will also be qualified to teach others." Thus the process, for Paul, was to take the things that he had taught publicly (presence of many witnesses), and to have Timothy (the reader), the disciple or entrust those things to "reliable men" who would then pass those truths on to others. **Four generations** of discipleship are involved in that single verse. This is sort of like a divine stacking process that has eternal benefits.

But discipleship is much more than that. When Jesus said, "If anyone would be my disciple, let him deny himself, take up his cross and follow me," he was advocating discipleship—and also the costs involved. For centuries, this has been a rich concept, but it was rediscovered with a vengeance in the second half of the 20th century. Let's hope that it continues to be passed on in the 21st century.

Dietrich Bonhoeffer lived from 1906-1945—a life shortened by martyrdom at the hand of the Nazis. He was a German pastor.[48] The child of a famous neurologist, he studied philosophy and theology at Tubingen and Berlin, coming under the influence of such men as Deissmann, Harnack, Lietzmann, Seeberg, and Karl Barth.

Bonhoeffer was born into an upper class family characterized by wealth and sophistication on February 4, 1906; he was the sixth of eight children. The family on both sides had been part of Germany's well-connected, well-educated cultural elite.

Despite his parents' nominal Christian commitment, a wide range of virtues were inculcated in the Bonhoeffer home that would later bear fruit in Dietrich's life: moral responsibility,

---

[48] Source for this section of his biography is the *NIDCC*, 141-142.

concern for the needs of others, intellectual objectivity, critical thinking, personal integrity, self-discipline, and high expectations of self and others. The family opposed Hitler from the beginning, and during the Nazi regime many members became involved in resistance activities.

Dietrich Bonhoeffer, an impossibly precocious student, zoomed through school, completing his University of Berlin doctoral dissertation (The Communion of the Saints) at 21 (a work Karl Barth called "a theological miracle") and a second dissertation (Act and Being) at 23. His promise as a theologian was obvious. As John De Gruchy has written, "Had he lived longer he might have dominated the theological scene in the second half of the twentieth century." Because of his historical context, and choices he made within that context, his contributions have emerged in ways altogether unanticipated by the bright young theologian in 1929.

Even then, Bonhoeffer recognized the basic choice he faced, to follow the conventional path of comfort and "successful" ministry in the Christian "religion," or instead to follow Jesus Christ the living Lord in the midst of a collapsing culture and a faithless church. Perhaps this is why, unlike so many of this colleagues, he was prepared to give up the security of the state-approved churches and universities early in the Nazi era rather than compromise his conscience by remaining in nazified institutions. Bonhoeffer renounced the lure of short-term success in the name of fidelity to Jesus Christ.

Ordained as a Lutheran pastor, he ministered to German congregations in Barcelona and London and took a leading part in drafting the *Barmen Declaration*, a 1935 document that confronted the Nazi's totalitarian claims. He thus became a leader of the Confessing Church (not the state-supported/funded church) which refused the Aryan Clauses (1933) imposed by the Nazi ideology.

The seminary which Bonhoeffer founded for training pastors for the Confessing Church was short-lived; his license to teach was revoked in 1936; Himmler closed the seminary in 1937. Even though his theology was thoroughly modern in some respects, he also lived out the ancient discipleship called for by Jesus.

Bonhoeffer opposed Hitlerism which thrust him into the Resistance movement and led to his arrest by the Gestapo in April 1943. He was executed, on a charge of treason; a simple tablet in the village church is inscribed: "Dietrich Bonhoeffer a witness of Jesus Christ among his brethren."

His later works which have been translated into English include *The Cost of Discipleship* (1948); *Letters and Papers from Prison* (1953); *Life Together* (1954); *Creation and Fall* (1959); *No Rusty Swords* (1965); *Christology* (1966), among others.

Sadly, Bonhoeffer followed much of the liberal German theology in the early 20th century. Still, among his most fruitful insights were his total rejection of natural theology, and of a "religious *apriori*" in man; the reality of God's absolute self-disclosure in Christ; the historical and present Christ as God revealed incognito . . ."

However, he remained faithful in a time of testing to follow Jesus Christ. Bonhoeffer, even with certain theological inconsistencies, remembered Jesus' call to follow him, even if it meant suffering, opposition, or death. In his obedience, he inspired many.

What did Jesus say about discipleship?

In the early chapters of John, we see discipleship front and center; in fact, Jesus' whole ministry was involved with discipleship. John the Baptist had disciples; so these were not Jesus' invention. The disciples of John lived with him, learned from him, walked with him, observed him, and were loyal to him. When Jesus came on the scene some of John's disciples began to follow him. In John 1:32, we see two of John's disciples. When Jesus passes by, John points his disciples to Jesus. They begin to follow Jesus (1:37) and spend the day with him. These were Andrew (Peter's brother) and Philip. Both of these then bring others to Christ. That is discipleship: Knowing Christ and leading others to the best thing in life.

One of Jesus' first works was to call the disciples. He assembled 12 and they followed him around. They saw his reactions and impulses, they heard his teaching, and they watched his miracles; at times, they were even involved in miracles (Philip in John 6). They learned from him, verbally and non-verbally. They apparently had no fixed headquarters and lived in poverty. But these disciples knew that poverty with Jesus was better than riches with anyone else.

These were in training to carry on the mission of Christ. They had to learn from the Master. He also taught them that the life of discipleship would not necessarily be easy; that is a major lesson of discipleship. Bonhoeffer claimed, "When Christ calls a man, he bids him come and die." "There are different kinds of dying," admitted the late Bishop of Chichester, G. K. A. Bell, "but the essence of discipleship is contained in those words." Bonhoeffer also knew that the life of discipleship "would be joy" and "a road of boundless mercy."

Turn your attention to Luke 9:57-62.

The disciples had just completed an argument about who was the greatest among them (Lk. 9:46-50). Can you believe that those so close to Jesus would be so petty? Still happens, I'm afraid to admit. Shortly after that, Jesus was rejected in a Samaritan village. He and his disciples are enroute to another village. While they were walking on the road, a man approached and wanted to enlist to follow Jesus. The man expressed, "I will follow you wherever you go." Jesus, however, did not accept this man's enlistment. It may be because Jesus knew that he had not properly counted the costs for discipleship. Jesus responded, "Foxes have holes and birds of the air have nests, but the Son of Man has no place to lay his head." He was telling this would-be follower that even the lowest of the animal kingdom had a place to call their own at night, but that Jesus had no place to call home. If the disciple was not above the Master, and if Jesus was the Master, then this meant that the disciples had no places of their own, and that any follower needed to be prepared for that. I wonder if we are prepared for that? I wonder if we were walking alongside of Jesus today, would we follow him in view of the high costs?

Another inquirer then initiates a conversation with Jesus. The second questioner is summoned: "Follow me." This man has what appears to be an urgent task to complete first. He says, "Lord, let me first go and bury my father." There are 2 schools of interpretation on the question of why this was unacceptable to Jesus. It was clearly rejected by Jesus' words, "Let the dead bury their own dead, but you go and proclaim the kingdom of God." One school of thought on this verse sees this second candidate as expressing a will to follow Christ, but not any time soon. The phrase "bury my father," could in some contexts mean, "Let me take care of him from now on until he dies (**could be years**), and then I will bury my father. If that was the case, Jesus knew that this man did not want to be a disciple anytime soon; just when it was convenient or when he got around to it; or if his father wasn't too old, then maybe never. Jesus saw through that and rejected that. Some people today want to be disciples of Jesus whenever they get good and ready to.

Another school of thought sees a very radical claim. Jesus had taught that even one's parents were not to be elevated over the call to obedience. The second school of thought thinks that this man's father had died and it would be only a matter of days before this man could follow Jesus. If that were the case, Jesus may seem harsh, but in reality he is stressing the need to follow Christ and to do so quickly. Either interpretation makes it clear: Jesus will not be our second priority.

Bonhoeffer saw this clearly and said that the disciple looked only to Christ as Master; never to the world or even to religion. He also noted: "Everything which hinders us from loving God above all things and acts as a barrier between ourselves and our obedience to Jesus is our treasure, and the place where our heart is." [49] Our hearts must be given entirely to God. We cannot serve two competing Masters.

A little later in the same gospel, Jesus told a parable in Luke 14:25-33. When large crowds began to follow him, Jesus made it

---

[49] Dietrich Bonhoeffer, *The Cost of Discipleship* (New York: Macmillan, 1975) 194. All references unless otherwise noted to this edition.

clear that if a person did not have greater love for him than for his parents and friends, then that person could not be his disciple. It is in this context that Jesus spoke of cross-bearing. He said that if a person did not carry a cross and follow him, he could not be his disciple. Then Jesus launched into a parable.

This parable was about a building contractor. This builder will first make estimates and calculate how much money he has and how much money the project may cost. The experienced builder will not set out, start laying foundation and brick, only to discover that he does not have the expertise or finances to complete the project. Not merely in the world of wish fulfillment, but in the world of real prospects, a person assesses as much as possible whether or not he can do a job prior to beginning. If we see that we do not have the resources, then we must wait. Similarly, the costs of discipleship must be calculated first.

Likewise, if one cannot complete a project, or if one does not have the resources or will to carry through, one ought to wait until he does. This is basic economics but also basic spirituality. God calls you to count the costs, too; and to go ahead and follow Jesus. If we first count the costs, then we might not be so easily discouraged. Expect, Jesus taught, difficulty. Be prepared for it.

Jesus expected his messengers and disciples to suffer. Bonhoeffer spoke of it this way. "The cross is laid on every Christian. The first Christ-suffering which every man must experience is the call to abandon the attachments of this world." (99)

Jesus and Bonhoeffer agreed about another thing: he taught against what he called 'cheap grace.' Cheap grace was, for him and to us, "the deadly enemy of our Church." He opposed the view that one could take, take, take from the Church and never give. Christ gave grace, but not lethargy. Cheap grace was the proclamation of the forgiveness of sins as the only general truth of Christianity; it depended on the conception of God as only loving and forgiving— never calling us to suffering. "Cheap grace means the justification of sin without the justification of the sinner. Cheap grace is not the kind of forgiveness of sin which frees us from the toils of sin.

Cheap grace is the grace we bestow on ourselves. Cheap grace is grace without discipleship, grace without the cross, grace without Jesus Christ." (46-47) In contrast, "Costly grace is the treasure hidden in the field; for the sake of it a man will gladly go and sell all that he has." It is costly because it involves the cost of the life of God's own Son.

Discipleship is a life that understands the value of Christ's death. It does not take grace for granted. It estimates the cost as infinite. Discipleship is passing on to another person the meaning of Christ's death and how to live as a follower of Christ.

Many other passages illustrate this concept of discipleship.

- In the OT for example, Moses discipled Joshua; he took him under his wing and taught him to be his successor.
- Elijah discipled Elisha; so did other prophets. Later in the NT, Paul discipled Timothy, Luke, Titus, and others.

What happens when the costs are not counted? A NT illustration is the case of John Mark. Young Mark deserted Paul on his first missionary journey. Paul sent him home and would not go with him again, apparently because Mark lost his nerve. He had not counted the costs, and when the going got tough, Mark got going . . . home. The Christian life does have some difficulties attached to it, and those must be fairly considered as part of the core of faith. It is a regular part of biblical Christianity to count the costs prior to embarking.

Have you ever been in a restaurant and discovered you didn't have enough money to pay the bill? When you discover that (and its potential embarrassment, especially if you are seeking to impress a date or a client), you may wish that you had counted the costs first. If we arrive somewhere and owe some money, and do not have it, it is very uncomfortable. But we will survive, and that is a relatively minor thing. Even more important is it to count the costs for an eternal relationship. Have you ever known a person who started off a Christian life with a bang, only to finish with a whimper? Or do you know Christians who have great goals, but never quite seem to attain them? Sometimes I'm that way. Sometimes, when ideas are not yet clothed with flesh, they seem so easy, so attainable, but then in reality, they may be much more difficult. We should count the costs first.

Jesus calls you to be one of his disciples. Bonhoeffer in this the *Cost of Discipleship* mentors us as below:

The kind of discipleship that Jesus expects from us is the one that will "rely on Christ's word and cling to it as offering greater security than all the securities in the world." (87) A Christian is called to "deny oneself . . . to be aware only of Christ and no more of self, to see only him who goes before and no more the road which is too hard for us." (97) Bonhoeffer also acknowledged that grace must come first: "Obedience to the call of Jesus never lies within our own power." (93)

Some people will even become disciples of some idea or religion or method that is not that of Jesus. It is easy to become disciples of one's own religion. Why, it is even possible to become disciples of the self-god.

Matthew 19:16-22 exhibits an example of the Rich Young Ruler who wanted to follow Christ but to do it his way. He seemed to volunteer to serve with Jesus, but when confronted, he found that it was more difficult than he had anticipated. Why, Jesus did not want some token of commitment; he wanted our whole soul.

Every member of our church is asked 5 basic vows. The third one asks about a life of discipleship: "Will you promise, depending upon the grace of the Holy Spirit to live a life as becoming of a follower of Christ." That calls us all to discipleship.

Spurgeon At his best (p. 59) said it well: "If persecution should arise, you should be willing to part with all that you possess—with your liberty, with your life itself, for Christ—or you cannot be his disciple."

Let me make one final point about discipleship. I was once having a discussion with an elder; we were talking about our children. We both agreed on something: Many of life's most important lessons are those that are learned from observation, or even non-verbally. Discipleship is far more than a series of tutorials. Discipleship is not merely meeting to pass on knowledge, although it involves that. It is also living together and learning from other mature Christians how to handle the situations of life. For example, in a family, it may be that hundreds of hours in a lifetime are spent in family devotionals. Children will likely not remember all the content discussed. They will remember this: the family believes, prays, takes time for the important things, looks to God for guidance, etc. These are some of the most important lessons in life. Similarly, in the church, much learning occurs as young Christians watch and live with older Christians. Some of the most important truisms are caught not taught.

Think of what you have learned from other Christians. A young relative once shared his life plan with me. Unexpectedly, this 10th grader blurted out: 'He wanted to attend a Christian College, major in Bible, and return to teach Bible to High School students." I was shocked.

Now where did that come from? Not from me, not even from his mother who loves the Lord. Best I can tell, he has an elder at his church who is a superb Bible-teacher, and probably unknown to that teacher, this young man wants to pattern his life—in some respects—after him. That's discipleship—passing on what is truly important about the Lord through example. What are you passing on to your children and those around you? You ARE conveying something.

I believe that if we are living with the Lord as we should that we will always have some things to share with other disciples. There should be a certain overflow in which we graciously share the practice of Christian living with others. It ought also to be somewhat natural and unplanned. Real lessons of discipleship are often "caught" more than "taught." Disciples look at our lives, judge our responses, and during stress, our real values are made clear. Jesus passed on those deep values to his disciples, and among the primary lessons were: following him would be costly, and at times difficult. Discipleship involved bearing the cross. Like Jesus, the disciple must die to self—and to its goals, ambitions, and desires. The tough times are part of discipleship.

One historian writing about the explorer Sir Francis Drake described how Drake's sailors would sit on the rocks off the rugged coast of England telling stories of the sea to the young country boys who would gather around to listen. The sailors did not talk of the pleasures of the sea, but of the **dangers**—raging winds, the stout waves and the gallant ships riding out the storms. After hearing the captivating tales many boys ran away from home to be part of them. It was the difficulty that summoned them; not the ease or comfort.

The call to discipleship that Jesus gives is not a summons to a life of comfort and ease, but to a life-style of risk and involvement. Jesus never hides his scars from a prospective follower. He calls out the best in people, and he touches something deep in our human nature.

One of the important truths of our lives is that we must have a purpose and commitment to be vital. Our commitments focus our lives and energize us. What we receive from our faith seems to be in proportion to what we have given.

In his call, Jesus does not give people the option of straddling the fence or holding back. He knows the strength of a clear commitment."

He calls us to count the costs, and to value those costs as minimal compared to the unfading glory of knowing him and being known. Do count the costs, but move on and follow Christ, even if it involves death.

Chapter 13

The Mystery of the Lord's Supper (Thomas Watson)

Matthew 26:26-28

The Greeks call the sacrament "a mystery." At times, what happens here does exceed our comprehension. There is in it a mystery of wonder and a mystery of mercy. "The celebration of the Lord's Supper," said Chrysostom, "is the commemoration of the greatest blessing that ever the world enjoyed." A sacrament is a visible sermon. The Word is a trumpet to proclaim Christ. The sacrament is a glass to represent Him.

The Word is for the engrafting; the Sacraments are for the confirming of faith. The Word brings us to Christ; the Sacrament builds us up in Him. The Lord condescends to our weakness. Were we made up purely of spirit, there would be no need of bread and wine. But we are compound creatures. Therefore God, to help our faith, not only gives us an audible word but a visible sign. Our Savior acknowledged, "Except you see signs, you will not believe" (John 4:48). Christ sets His body and blood before us in the elements. Here are signs, [to confirm our belief].

So as we come to our text in Mt. "As they were eating, Jesus took bread," I wish to highlight five particulars (from T Watson) in reference to the Sacrament:

1. The Author.
2. The Time.
3. The Manner.
4. The Guests.
5. The Benefits.

1. The Author of the Sacrament, Jesus Christ. "Jesus took bread." To institute sacraments belongs, by right, to Christ, and is a flower of His crown. Only He who can give grace can appoint the sacraments, which are the seals of grace. Christ, being the Founder of the Sacrament, gives a glory and luster to it. Always remember that Jesus is the sole Author of this sacrament. Next:

2. The time when Christ instituted the Sacrament;

1. It was "after supper," Luke 22:20, to show that the Sacrament is chiefly intended as a spiritual banquet. It was not to indulge the senses, but to feast the graces. It was "after supper"

2. Also Christ appointed the Sacrament shortly before His sufferings. "The Lord Jesus, the same night in which He was betrayed, took bread," 1 Corinthians *11:23.* He knew troubles were soon coming upon His disciples. It would be no small perplexity to them to see their Lord and Master crucified. And shortly afterwards they must pledge to follow Him in a bitter cup. Therefore, to arm them against such a time and to animate their spirits, that very night in which He was betrayed He gives them mysteriously His body and blood in the Sacrament.

This may give us a good hint that, in all trouble of mind, especially approaches of danger, it is needful to have recourse to the Lord's Supper. The Sacrament is both an antidote against fear and a restorative to faith. The night in which Christ was betrayed, He took bread.

3. The manner of the institution;

1. The taking of the bread. "Jesus took bread." Why did Christ take bread rather than any other element?

ANSWER 1. Because it prefigured him. Christ was typified by the show bread, 1 Kings 7:48; by the bread which Melchisedek offered unto Abraham, Genesis 14:18; and by the cake which the angel brought to Elijah, 1 Kings 19:6. Therefore, He took bread to answer the type [from years of OT preparation].

ANSWER 2. Christ took bread also because of the analogy. Bread resembled Him closely. "I am that Bread of life," John 6:48. There is a three-fold resemblance:

Bread is useful. Other comforts are more for delight than use. Music delights the ear, colors the eye, but bread is the staff of life. So Christ is useful. There is no subsisting without Him. "He that eateth Me, even he shall live by Me, "John 6:57.

Bread is satisfying. If a man is hungry, flowers or pictures do not satisfy, but bread does. So Jesus Christ, the Bread of the soul, satisfies. He satisfies the eye with beauty, the heart with sweetness, the conscience with peace.

Bread is strengthening. "Bread which strengthens man's heart," Psalm 104:15. So Christ, the Bread of the soul, transmits strength. He strengthens us against temptations and for doing and suffering work.

2. *Also* When Christ was bruised on the cross, He sent out a fragrant smell. Christ's body crucifying was the breaking open of a box of precious ointment which filled heaven and earth with its perfume.

Why, then, was His blessed body broken? It was for our sins. "He was wounded for our transgressions," Isaiah 53:5. The Hebrew word for "wounded" has a double emphasis. Either it may signify that He was pierced through as with a dart, or that He was profaned. He was used as some common vile thing, and Christ can thank us for it. "He was wounded for our transgressions." It was our sins that smote Him. Our pride made Christ wear a crown of thorns. Christ could say to His church, "A bloody spouse you have been to Me; you have cost Me My heart's blood."

Now, concerning Christ's suffering upon the cross, observe these things:

The bitterness of it to Him. "He was broken." The very thoughts of His suffering put Him into an agony. "Being in agony, He prayed more earnestly, and He sweat, as it were, great drops of blood falling down to the ground," Luke 22:44. He was full of sorrow. "My soul is exceeding sorrowful, even unto death," Matthew 26:38. Christ's crucifixion was: 1. A lingering death. *It was more for Christ to suffer one hour than for us to have suffered forever.* But His death was lengthened out. He hung three hours on the cross. He died many deaths before He could die one.

2. It was a painful death. His hands and feet were nailed; these parts, being full of sinews, were therefore very tender, His pain must be most acute and sharp. And to have the envenomed arrow of God's wrath shot to His heart, this was the direful catastrophe, and caused that outcry upon the cross, "My God, My God, why hast Thou forsaken Me?" The justice of God was now enflamed and heightened to its full. "God spared not His Son," Romans 8:38. Nothing must be abated of the debt. Christ felt the pains of hell; In the Sacrament's mystery, we see this tragedy acted before us.

3. It was a shameful death. Christ was hung between two thieves, Matthew 27:38. It was as if He had been the principal malefactor. Well might the lamp of heaven withdraw its light and mask itself with darkness, as blushing to behold the Sun of righteousness in an eclipse. It is hard to say which was greater—the blood of the cross or the shame of the cross, Hebrews 12:2.

4. It was a cursed death, Deuteronomy 21:23. This kind of death was deemed exceedingly despicable, yet the Lord Jesus underwent

this, "Being made a curse for us," Galatians 3:13. He who was God blessed forever, Romans 9:5, was under a curse.

Calvin calls the crucifixion of Christ the hinge on which our salvation turns. Luther calls it a gospel spring opened to refresh sinners. Indeed, the suffering of Christ is a deathbed cordial. It is an antidote to expel all our fear. Does sin trouble? Christ has overcome it for us. Besides the two thieves crucified with Christ, there were two other invisible thieves crucified with Him: sin and the devil. [Review]

4. The fourth thing is the guests invited to this supper, or the persons to whom Christ distributed the elements. "He gave to His disciples and said, Take, eat." The Sacrament is children's bread. If a man makes a feast, he calls his friends. Christ calls His disciples; if He had any piece better than another, He carves it to them.

"This is My body which is given for you," Luke 22:19, that is, for you believers. Christ gave His body and blood to the disciples chiefly under this notion, that they were believers. As Christ poured out His prayers, John 17:9, so His blood only for believers. See how near to Christ's heart all believers lie! Christ's body was broken on the cross and His blood shed for them. Christ has passed by others, and died intentionally for his elect. Impenitent sinners have no benefit by Christ's death unless it is a short reprieve. Christ is given to the wicked in wrath. He is a Rock of offence, 1 Pet 2:8. Christ's blood is like drops of oil which recover some patients, but kill others. Judas sucked death from the tree of life. God can turn stones into bread, and a sinner can turn bread into stones-the bread of life into the stone of stumbling.

5. The fifth thing observable in the text is the benefit of this supper in these words, "for the remission of sins." This is a mercy of the first magnitude, the crowning blessing. "Who forgiveth thy iniquities, who crowneth thee with loving-kindness," Psalm 103:3-4. Whosoever has this charter granted is enrolled in the book of life. "Blessed is he whose transgression is forgiven," Psalm 32:1. Under this word, "remission of sin," is comprehended all heavenly benedictions, justification, adoption, and glory—which led Chrysostom to call this Supper "the feast of the cross."

USE   2.   It   informs   us   of   several   things. *1. It shows us the necessity of coming to the Lord's Supper.* Has Jesus Christ gone to all this cost to make a feast? Then, surely, there must be guests, Luke 22:19. It is not left to our choice whether we will come or not; it is an indispensable duty. The words "Let him eat of that bread," (1 Cor 11:28) are not only permissive, but authoritative. It is as if a king should say, "Let it be enacted."

The neglect of the Sacrament runs men into a gospel penalty. It was infinite goodness in Christ to broach that blessed vessel of His body and let His sacred blood stream out. It is evil for us wilfully to omit such an ordinance wherein the trophy of mercy is so richly displayed and our salvation so nearly concerned. Well may Christ take this as an undervaluing of Him, and interpret it as no better than a bidding Him to keep His feast to Himself. He who did not observe the passover was to be cut off, Numbers 9:13. How angry was Christ with those who stayed away from the supper! They thought to put it off with a compliment. But Christ knew how to construe their excuse for a refusal. "None of those men which were bidden shall taste of My supper," Luke 14:24. Rejecting gospel mercy is a sin so deep that God can do no less than punish it for a contempt. Some need a flaming sword to keep them from the Lord's Table, and others need Christ's whip of small cords to drive them to it.

3. See in this text, as in a glass, infinite love displayed. THE MYSTERY SHOWN

(1) Behold the love of God the Father in giving Christ to be broken for us. That God should put such a jewel in pledge is the admiration of angels. "God so loved the world that He gave His

only begotten Son," John 3:16. It is a pattern of love without a parallel. It was a far greater expression of love in God to give His Son to die for us than if He had voluntarily acquitted us of the debt without any satisfaction at all. If a subject is disloyal to his sovereign, it argues more love in the king to give his own son to die for that subject than to forgive him the wrong freely.

(2) That Christ should suffer death. "Lord," said Bernard, "Thou hast loved me more than thyself; for you laid down your life for me." Christ ripped off His own flesh for us. That Christ should die as the greatest sinner, having the weight of all men's sins laid upon Him, here is most transporting love! It sets all the angels in heaven wondering.

(3) That Christ should die freely. "I lay down My life," John 10:17. There was no law to enjoin Him, no force to compel Him. It is called the offering of the body of Jesus, Hebrews 10:10. What could fasten Him to the cross but the golden link of love!

(4) That Christ should die for such as we are. What are we? Not only vanity, but enmity! When we were fighting, He was dying. **When He had the weapons in our hands, then He had the spear in His side,** Romans 5:8.

(5) That Christ died for us when He could not expect to be at all bettered by us. We were reduced to penury. We were in such a condition that we could neither merit Christ's love nor requite it. For Christ to die for us when we were at such a low ebb was the very quintessence of love. One man will extend kindness to another as long as he is able to requite him. But if he is fallen to decay, then love begins to slacken and cool. But when we were engulfed in misery and fallen to decay, when we had lost our beauty, stained our blood, and spent our portion, then Christ died for us. O amazing love, which may swallow up all our thoughts!

(6) That Christ should not retreat from His sufferings. "He shall see the travail of His soul and shall be satisfied," Isaiah 53:11. It is a metaphor that alludes to a mother who, though she has suffered

greatly, does not retreat from it when she sees a child brought
forth. So, though Christ had hard travail upon the cross, yet he
does not shrink from it, but thinks all his sufferings well-bestowed.
He shall be satisfied. The Heb word signifies such a satiating as a
man has at some sweet repast or banquet.

(7) That Christ should rather die for us than the angels that fell.
They were creatures of a more noble extraction and, in all
probability, might have brought greater revenues of glory to God,
Yet, that Christ should pass by those golden vessels and make us
clods of earth into stars of glory, O the **hyperbole** of Christ's
love!

(8) Yet another step of Christ's love, for like the waters of the
sanctuary it rises higher: that Christ's love should not cease at the
hour of death! Christ died once, but loves forever. He is not merely
testifying His affection to us. He is also making the mansions
ready for us, John 14:2. He is interceding for us, Hebrews 7:25. He
appears in the court as the Advocate for the client. **When He has
finished dying, yet He has not finished loving**. What a
stupendous love was here! Who can meditate upon this and not be
in ecstasy? Well may the apostle call it "a love that passes
knowledge," Ephesians 3:19. When you see Christ broken in the
Sacrament, think of this love's mystery. It is beyond our grasp!

*4. See, then, what dear and entire affections we should bear to
Christ, who gives us His body and blood in the eucharist.* If he had
had anything to part with of more worth, he would have bestowed
it upon us. O let Christ lie nearest our hearts! Let him be our Tree
of Life, and let us desire no other fruit. Let him be our morning
Star, and let us rejoice in no other light.

As Christ's beauty, so his bounty should make him loved by us. He
has given us his blood as the price and his Spirit as the witness of
our pardon. In the Sacrament, Christ bestows all good things. He
both imputes his righteousness and imparts his lovingkindness. He
gives a foretaste of that supper which shall be celebrated in the

paradise of God. To sum up all, in the blessed supper, Christ gives himself to believers, and what can he give more?

In this, we view sin odious in the red glass of Christ's sufferings. It is true, sin is to be abominated since it turned Adam out of paradise and threw the angels down to hell. *Sin is the peace-breaker*. It is like an incendiary in the family that sets husband and wife at variance. It makes God fall out with us. Sin is the birthplace of our sorrows and the grave of our comforts. But that which may most of all disfigure the face of sin and make it appear abominable is this: It crucified our Lord! It made Christ veil His glory and lose His blood.

Was Christ's body broken? Let us, then, from His suffering on the cross, learn this lesson not to wonder much if we meet with troubles in the world. Did Christ suffer who "knew no sin," and do we think it strange to suffer who know nothing but sin? Did Christ feel the anger of God? And is it much for us to feel the anger of men? Was the Head crowned with thorns? Must we have our bracelets and diamonds when Christ had the spear and nails going to His heart? Truly, such as are guilty may well expect the lash when He, who was innocent, could not go free.

Let us be moved by the great goodness of Christ. Who can tread upon these hot coals and his heart not burn? If a friend should die for us, would not our hearts be much affected with his kindness? That the God of heaven should die for us, how should this stupendous mercy have a melting influence upon us! The body of Christ broken is enough to break the most flinty heart. At our Savior's passion, the very stones cleaved asunder. "The rocks rent," Matthew 27:51. He who is not affected with this has a heart harder than the stones. How can we not be affected with Christ's kindness who, to spare our life, lost His own! Let us pray that, as Christ was fastened to the cross, so He may be fastened to our hearts.

Let us prize Christ's blood in the Sacrament. It is drink indeed, John 6:55. Here is the nectar and ambrosia God Himself delights to taste of. This is both a balsam and a perfume. And a mystery!

Finally, know the SEVEN SUPERNATURAL VIRTUES IN CHRIST'S BLOOD

That we may set the higher value upon the blood of Christ. I close with 7 aspects of mystery in Christ's blood:

1. It is a reconciling blood. 'You that were sometime alienated, and enemies, yet now hath He reconciled through death," Col 1:21. Christ's blood is the blood of atonement.

2. Christ's blood is a quickening blood. "Whoso drinketh My blood, hath eternal life," John 6:54. It both begets life and prevents death.

3. Christ's blood is a cleansing blood. "How much more shall the blood of Christ purge your conscience!" Hebrews 9:14. As the merit of Christ's blood pacifies God, so the virtue of it purifies us. It is the King of heaven's bath.

4. Christ's blood is a softening blood. There is nothing so hard but may be softened by this blood. It will soften a stone.

5. Christ's blood cools the heart. First, it cools the heart of sin. The heart naturally is full of distempered heat. It burns in lust and passion. Christ's blood allays this heart and quenches the inflammation of sin. Second, it cools the heat of conscience. It times of desertion, conscience burns with the heat of God's displeasure. When the heart burns and is in agony, Christ's blood is like water to the fire. It has a cooling, refreshing virtue in it.

6. Christ's blood comforts the soul. Christ's blood is best in affliction. It cures the trembling of the heart.

A conscience sprinkled with Christ's blood can, like the nightingale, sing with a thorn at its breast. The blood of Christ

can make a prison become a palace. It turned the martyr's flames into beds of roses. Christ's blood gives comfort at the hour of death. As a holy man once said on his death-bed when they brought him a cordial, "No cordial like the blood of Christ!"

7. Christ's blood procures heaven. So, through the red sea of Christ's blood, we enter into the heavenly Canaan. Our sins shut heaven; Christ's blood is the key which opens the gate of paradise for us. Thus, Theodoret calls the cross the tree of salvation because that blood which trickled down the cross distils salvation. Well, then, may we prize the blood of Christ and, with Paul, determine to know nothing but Christ crucified, 1 Cor 2:2]

BRANCH 3. IF Christ offers his body and blood to us in the Supper, then with what solemn preparation should we come to so sacred an ordinance! The heart must be prepared and put in tune before it goes to meet with God in this solemn ordinance of the Sacrament. Take heed of rashness or irreverence. If we do not come prepared, we do not drink but spill Christ's blood. We read of a wine cup of fury in God's hand, Jer 25:15. He that comes unprepared to the Lord's Supper turns the cup in the Sacrament into a cup of fury.

Oh, with what reverence and devotion should we address ourselves to these holy mysteries! The saints are called "prepared vessels," (Rom 9:23). If ever these vessels should be prepared, it is when they are to hold the precious body and blood of Christ. The sinner who is damned is first prepared. Men do not go to hell without some kind of preparation. "Vessels fitted for destruction," Rom 9:22. If those vessels are prepared which are filled with wrath, much more are those to be prepared who are to receive Christ in the Sacrament. Let us dress ourselves by a Scripture glass before we come to the Lord's Table and, with the Lamb's wife, make ourselves ready.

MYSTERY; Tis Mystery All!

Made in the
USA
Columbia, SC